A POLICE DOG HANDLER'S STORY

BY

BRYN PHILLIPS

With my best wishes to my dear friends Mike + Anne.

Bryn Phillips

NEW MILLENNIUM

292 Kennington Road, London SE11 4LD

British Library Cataloguing in Publication Data.
A catalogue record for this book is available
from the British Library.

Printed and bound by Watkiss Studios Ltd.
Biggleswade, Beds.
Issued by New Millennium*
Set in 12 point Times New Roman Typeface
ISBN 1 85845 250 3
*An imprint of The Professional Authors' & Publishers' Association

DEDICATION

I dedicate this book to my wife Sybil, for the love and support she has given me for the last 50 years.

CONTENTS

CONTENTS

List of Photographs

Introduction

When I was coming to the end of writing these memoirs, I was appalled on reading in the national press of the incident of cruelty to police dogs in the Essex Dog Section. What happened was an absolute disgrace and cannot be excused in any way.

I was hurt and disappointed by reader's letters to the press, typifying all police dog handlers with this kind of treatment to their dogs.

For twenty-four-years of my police service from the rank of constable to Chief Inspector I was fully engaged in the training of police dogs. I travelled extensively in this country and abroad in the capacity of instructor, judge and assessor of police dogs and I can say with hand on my heart that not once did I see or hear of any form of cruelty to any of the dogs.

Anyone who has attended police dog trials would have seen the dogs walking beside their handlers with a springy gait, tails wagging and looking up at the handler, eager for the next command. Does anyone think that this kind of behaviour is achieved by the dog with the use of cruelty or punishment?

Any success in dog training can only be achieved when there is a strong bond of trust and affection between dog and handler and I can say without any doubt, that the incident in Essex is the exception rather than the rule.

The author

CHAPTER ONE
MY EARLY DAYS

When I turned my car into the driveway of Staffordshire Police Headquarters on that Sunday afternoon in September 1963, and sa w for the first time the police dog training area, with all the apparatus used for the training of the dogs, I glanced at my dog lying in the back of the car and said, 'Well, Abi girl, this is it!' Abi was a 11 month old German Shepherd bitch and we were just arriving to commence a 13 week Initial Dog Handlers Course at the Home Office Police Dog Training School, which was based at Stafford.

It was something that I had always wanted to do, and I felt that I had found my niche in life.

I also thought that this was the height of anything that life had in store for me, and to say that I was happy and satisfied was an understatement. If someone had been able to tell me what lay ahead in the years to come, I would not have believed them, and it would have been way beyond my wildest dreams.

I was born in the County town of Haverfordwest, Pembrokeshire on 5th July,1931, but only lived there for a short while, as in the same year my parents moved to live in Goodwick, in the north of the County, where my father had obtained a job as manager of a nursery, specialising in the growing of tomatoes and cucumbers. Just after the war started in 1939, the nursery changed hands and it was bought by a Mr Le Tissier, from Guernsey, who had come to Wales just before the Channel Islands had been occupied by the Germans. Mr Le Tissier retained my father as manager of the nursery until just before the end of the war, when he decided that he would be going back to Guernsey to live. When the nursery was put on the market, Mr Le Tissier said that he would give my father the first refusal, if he was interested in buying. My father, having managed the nursery for so long, decided that he would buy it, so it became the family business.

I am the second of a family of four boys. My eldest brother, Ivor, is a year and ten months older than me, and I have two other brothers, David, who is seven years younger than me, and Gwyn, who is ten years younger.

I was eight years of age when the war started, which means that during the war years, I was of an age when children go out to play and go through the learning process for adulthood.

We used to make our own entertainment and enjoy the simple things in life. Mischief, in those days, meant knocking on peoples' doors and running away. Not stealing, damaging property or physically harming people, which is almost the 'norm' today. Now, we have the 'do-gooders', who give the reason for today's behaviour as, 'They are bored, and have nothing to do.'

What a load of rubbish! There are more leisure facilities, recreation and other forms of entertainment in the country today, then there had ever been, and most of it available to all children.

What the heck did we have as kids? We didn't even have street lights to play under, because of the blackout. For those who don't remember the war, the blackout meant that no lights were to be visible at night-time. So all the windows had to be covered with dark material to prevent any lights showing.

No! I'll tell you what we had. We had a more caring society. We had parents and school teachers who cared about our futures and did the job they were supposed to do, and did it properly. We had family life, as it was meant to be, sitting together in the evenings and around the meal table, conversing with each other and identifying ourselves with each other's problems and understanding each other's needs. Today, one comes home, switches on the television, and invariably sees and hears what most of the time is sex, violence or crime of some sort. Obviously, unsuitable material for grown-ups, let alone children. Children today grow up in a society, seeing and hearing this type of behaviour and believing that is the normal way in which people should behave. Yes! We as a society are to be blamed for allowing standards to be lowered to what is a totally unacceptable level.

During the war years, the whole of Fishguard Bay was mined, as a precaution against invasion by the Germans. In places, you could see the mines, which looked like big oil drums down beneath the water, on the edge of the rocks. The harbour itself was out of bounds to the public and was patrolled by sentries with rifles, to prevent unauthorised entry. For quite some time, there were two mine sweepers based at the port. I remember they were called the 'Cape Nemenski' and the 'Barracuda', or something like that. They used to sweep the channel for mines every day, and at night they were berthed alongside the quay wall. As kids we used to crawl down amongst the rocks, below where the old lifeboat shed used to be, with the sentries patrolling above us, and go on board the mine sweepers, where the sailors would give us slabs of fruit cake and mugs of sweet tea. To us it was like Christmas, not that we would have had such luxuries because of the rationing.

Another thing I well remember, was all the buses used for transporting workers to and from the Armaments Depot at Trecwn. After worktime, the buses would be parked overnight in the yard of the Jubilee Hall (no longer there), not far from the railway station (again no longer there). Every evening, we would go into the empty buses and search for any money which may have been dropped by the workers. We would often find several pennies and half pennies, which, to us kids in those days, was a lot of money. Every summer, we would look forward to the annual Sunday School trip to Tenby. For us, it was like going to the end of the world. The well-off kids would probably have about six pence to a shilling (3 to 5p) to spend in Tenby, and the rest of us, if lucky, maybe a few pennies. For all that, we would have a lovely time because we never knew any different.

When I was at school, although it was only a primary school, a Physical Training Inspector used to visit the school every couple of years. On one of his visits, he showed us how he could stand on his hands. This made quite an impression on me and I never forgot it. In fact, although I was only about 9 or 10 years at the time, I was determined that one day I would be able to do the same. Because of this, I would practise every day and became as 'at home' on my hands, as I was on my feet.

3

I always enjoyed anything physical and with a bit of a challenge attached to it. Using the vaulting horse in physical training always gave me a thrill and I was always doing some sort of training to improve my balancing. I was also very keen on athletics and was always eager to compete in the school and youth club sports. In those days, many villages held their own annual sports day, with money prizes for some of the events. Most of them featured the mile and half mile, with something like £5 for first prize, £3 for second and £1 for third. That was a lot of money in those days and gave one quite some incentive to compete. I used to have a go at most of them and often won a few pounds. One year in the County Youth Sports, I competed in nine different events.

I left school at the age of 14 years, just when the war ended, and with no educational qualifications at all. The irony of it was, that I was quite good at school and really enjoyed it, but I also wanted to leave and start working. As it was, I went to work for my father in the family business and obviously thought that this was where my future lay. Having said that, I had probably been working for my father for less than 12 months, when I realised that what I was doing was not what I really wanted. Working in the big glasshouses day in and day out to me became very boring and I knew beyond doubt that this was not what I wanted out of life. Although that was the situation, it was actually another 13 years before I finished working for my father at the nursery.

Working at the nursery with my father and elder brother Ivor, we specialised in growing tomatoes in the summer and chrysanthemums in the winter. In those days there was a Tomato Marketing Board, which enforced restrictions on the growing and sale of tomatoes. It allowed us to sell only a certain quantity of our produce retail and all the remainder had to be sold to a wholesaler. All of the fruit had to be graded, and if we sold any above the retail quota allowed, we could be heavily fined. These restrictions would sometimes cause a certain amount of bad feeling with the locals when they would come to the nursery to buy tomatoes and we would have to tell them that we did not have any to sell, when they could see hundreds of full baskets in the packing shed, ready for transporting by rail to the wholesalers.

It was probably me, but I found the work very boring and repetitive. The same time each year we would set the seeds in trays and, when the seedlings were about two inches high, we would put them into four inch pots. Before doing this, all the earthenware pots (no plastic in those days) had to be thoroughly sterilised, as did the compost we used for potting. We made our own potting compost using ingredients, which my father had always used with success. The plants were then brought on in the propagating glasshouse, which was specially built for that purpose, with three separate compartments, the first very hot for when the seedlings were first potted, the second less hot and the third less hot again, where the plants were hardened off before being planted out into the big glasshouses. We grew thousands of plants each year for our own use, and thousands more for sale.

Towards the end of January each year, we would plant them out in the big glasshouses, which were heated from three separate furnaces, which were fired by anthracite coal. The coal would be delivered by rail in large trucks to the local railway station, then loaded into a hired lorry by hand and transported to the nursery. There were obviously several lorry loads in each truck.

It was hard work, but I saw it as breaking the monotony at the nursery.

The very hard winter which we had in 1947, with very heavy snow for several days, meant that we had to work through several nights, tending to the furnaces. It was crucial that the right temperature was maintained in all the glasshouses, or we could easily lose all our plants and our livelihood for the year. One of the nights, when I was on, it snowed so heavily all night, that next morning, it took me over an hour to get home, a distance which normally took me about ten minutes.

Towards the end of March each year we would be picking our first tomatoes. We were always the first in Wales, and knew this for a fact, from the Inspectors that came around from the

5

Tomato Marketing Board. Even in those days, the first tomatoes were fetching £1 per pound.

It was essential that we picked early, in order to get the best prices, as once the Dutch, Spanish and Canary Islands tomatoes came into the country, the prices would plummet.

We used to put new top soil in the glasshouses every second year, and sterilize the soil with formaldehyde the years in between. We would buy the new top soil from anyone starting a building site, load it into a hired lorry and transport it to the nursery. Using wheelbarrows, we would then take out all the old soil from each glasshouse and wheel in the new, hundreds of tons - believe me, it was hard work, but it kept one fit.

The hard work I did not mind. What I did mind, were the two things over which we had no control, and that was the weather and the fluctuating markets. When growing foodstuffs, especially tomatoes, it is not something that you can hold back if the price is not right on the day. You have to take the price that you are offered, and that's not my idea of doing things.

As far back as I remember, I always had a good rapport with animals, and during my school days spent much of my time in the countryside with my dog and ferrets. Most weekends I would be rabbiting, something which I certainly could not do today. I also had a couple of goats, which gave good milk. At least they say it is good, but I must admit I did not like it.

As much as I enjoy anything to do with animals, especially horses and dogs, I absolutely abhor fox hunting. There is no way that I see it as a sport.

Whenever the banning of fox hunting is discussed, they always put up the argument that if this was to happen, they would have to get rid of all the horses and hounds involved. I cannot agree with that. The hounds are following the spoor of the fox and the animal does not necessarily have to be in the view of the hounds for them to take up the chase. A drag scent could be laid, with a strong smelling lure in lieu of the fox, and perhaps a carcass thrown to the hounds at the end of the chase as an incentive. Animals learn by association, and the hounds could quickly be trained to hunt and chase, just as they do when a live fox is used. Surely, the thrill of riding the horses at full gallop, and seeing the hounds in full flight, would still present the same amount of enjoyment, without seeing a poor animal being torn to bits at the end.

After I'd been working for about 18 months, I bought my first horse, straight off the Welsh hills. It cost me a fortune - £16.

The horse had never seen a rope before, let alone been led on one with a headcollar. Getting the headcollar onto the horse at the start, was a battle itself. I then had to walk the horse home on a lead rope, a distance of 6-7 miles. Admittedly, it was mostly quiet roads, with nothing like the amount of traffic that we get today. It was a Saturday afternoon, and passing through Fishguard Square, which was quite busy, was a nightmare. Nevertheless, we got home safely, horse and myself.

My next job was to break-in and school the horse. I did this myself, from what I had learned by watching a local horse trainer, known as 'Joe the Jockey.' In about two weeks, I was able to ride the horse. I later sold it to a local gypsy called 'Black Sam' and bought my second horse, which was much bigger than my first one. On this horse, I gained much riding experience, but little did I realise then how invaluable this would be to me many years in the future, and how it would help to further my career.

Before having horses of my own, I had learned to ride on my friend Derek Hughes's pony.

Sadly, today, Derek is no longer with us. I remember once, for a dare, riding Derek's pony bare back at full gallop along a rough track from a nearby farm towards the village, and at the same time carrying a basket full of eggs in one hand. At the end of the ride, all of the eggs were still intact. Not a very professional method to learn horsemanship, but what a confidence builder.

One day in 1947, when visiting Whitesands beach with some friends, I saw a group of men and girls practising tumbling and balancing. Always eager to get involved in this type of activity, I wandered over to get a closer look at what they were doing. My enthusiasm probably drew their attention to the fact that I was showing more than the usual interest in them performing, and they invited me to have a go. Ever since my school days, I'd been practising hand-balancing and tumbling, and had become quite competent. After a couple of balances with them, I could see that they were as keen on me joining them as I was.

I discovered that they were a troupe of weight-lifters and acrobats run by a man called Tommy George, who was well known as the 'Welsh Sandow', and that they gave shows all over the County. Tommy, who was with the group that day, asked me if I wished to join the troupe, and you can imagine what my answer was. In no time, I was really involved.

The troupe trained in a Nissen hut at the rear of a pub in the village of Letterston, which was about five miles from my home. Becoming a member of the troupe involved a big part of my life and I used to cycle out to the gym in Letterston to train three or four times a week.

One of the troupe, Yorrie Evans, was a champion weight-lifter, and I soon caught the bug. All the weight training obviously did much to improve my hand balancing, and I was soon able to do perfect hand-to-hand balances, two man high. I also started competitive weight- lifting, and we used to compete in the Welsh League every Saturday.

Yorrie lived in a place called Blaenllyn, which is about seven miles from my home He had his own gym at his home and I would cycle out to train with him on the nights when I wasn't training at Letterston. It made no difference what the weather was, I would cycle to Blaenllyn or Letterston, rain or shine.

In 1948, I was runner-up in a competition organised by the British Amateur Weight-lifting Association to find Britains Best All-round Junior Weight-lifter, but, as always, my main ambition was to become a professional hand-balancer. With this in mind, I went away to London to train with an Hungarian troupe in order to improve my skill. Obviously, my parents did not approve of my ideas, and strongly let me know their views when I returned from London.

I was a regular member of the Youth Club in Goodwick, which was held in the school which I used to attend. The Youth

Leader was also the local Scout Master, and he asked me if I was prepared to take the scouts in Physical Training every couple of weeks. I was obviously delighted to do this, and in no time at all, I was roped in as Assistant Scout Master. The following year, the Scout Master dropped a bombshell when he told me that he was leaving the area and that he wanted me to take over as Scout Master. To be honest, although I was honoured at being asked, I wasn't all that keen, as it was really interfering a little with my training. But never being one to say no, I reluctantly agreed to take over until they could find someone more permanent. As it turned out, I was there until 1951, and I must say that I enjoyed it all. We used to have some very enjoyable evenings, especially outdoors and in the summertime, when we used to go camping in Saundersfoot and Brecon, where we used to meet up with and befriend other scout troops from all over Wales.

As well as running, I used to enjoy cycling very much. In the summer of 1948, four of my friends and myself decided to go to Ireland on a cycling holiday. My friends were Ken Grace, Derek Hughes, Dai Panting and Keith Shipton. We had saved our money all the year and thought that the cheapest way was to stay in Youth Hostels, so we all joined the Youth Hostels Association.

We set off from Fishguard on the cross-channel ferry to Rosslare. Probably, one of the things uppermost in our minds was the fact that, although food rationing was still in effect back home, it was not so in Ireland, so we intended to make the most of it, and I can assure you, we did.

On arrival at Rosslare, we headed northwards, and stayed the first night in Wexford. There was no Youth Hostel in Wexford so we had to stay at a bed and breakfast, the cheapest we could find. On our tour, we visited Enniscorthy, Gorey, Arklow, Wicklow, Bray and Dublin, where we stayed a couple of nights. In Dublin, we visited a weight-lifting club, and I did some lifting with some of the local weight-lifters.

From Dublin, we made our way inland, and then travelled down the centre of Ireland, ending up in Tramore. One of the

Youth Hostels at which we stayed on our way down to Tramore was in an old castle, said to be haunted. The Hostel was overbooked that night and some of us had to sleep in the big, old fashioned open fireplace. Different, but we enjoyed it. In Tramore we hired some horses and used to go galloping along the beach.

There were not youth hostels at every place we stayed, so we had to find the cheapest bed and breakfast that we could. Of course, at the youth hostels we had to cook our own food and, believe me, we made pigs of ourselves. We used to buy loads of bacon, eggs, sausages and butter, and finish off with tins of fruit and cream. These were things that we rarely, if ever, saw at home. It was like living in another world.

From Tramore, maybe because we had eaten so much, we caught the train back to Waterford and then cycled to Rosslare to catch the ferry back to reality. I obviously don't remember exact figures, but I know that I had little over £20 when I set off from home on the start of the holiday for something that would cost a small fortune today. Things were so different in those days. Even if you didn't have much money, you seemed to get along quite comfortably on the little you had. Oh, for those days back.

Bryn during his hand balancing days

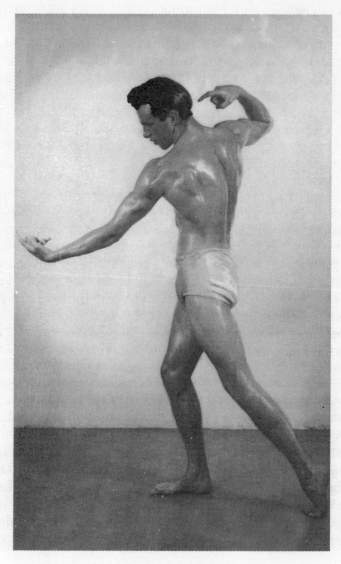

Bryn at 17 years

Many good things have happened to me in my life, but in 1949, when I was hell bent on becoming a professional hand-balancer, what I consider to be the best thing that ever happened to me was that I met Sybil, who was later to become my wife. Meeting her certainly changed my idea of going away in search of my dream and I realised that my mum and dad were right when persuading me that there was no future in what I wanted to do. Meeting Sybil, and changing my views, was a decision that I never regretted.

One weekend, when some of my friends had gone to Butlin's on holiday and I couldn't afford to go, I decided that I would go to Treherbert in the Rhondda Valley to see some friends that I had made at scout camp. Of course, the only way that I could afford to go was on my bicycle, so I set off early Saturday afternoon and cycled from Goodwick to Treherbert, stayed the night with my friends and cycled back on the Sunday - a distance of about 100 miles each way and without the good roads which we have today.

When I was a member of the troupe putting on shows for charity, we used to perform in halls all over the County and sometimes in adjoining Counties. In the troupe, there was Tommy, Yorrie, Yorrie's brother Lyn, three girls, Jean Morris, Betty Lawrence, Mary May, and of course myself. The performance would begin with some warm-up exercises. We would put on a balancing and tumbling routine, and then Tommy would perform some strong-man feats. Yorrie would then give a demonstration of Olympic weight-lifting, and we would finish off with a weight-lifting competition and invite members of the audience to join in.

One of my party pieces was to do diving rolls over the three girls who were kneeling down on all fours in front of the gymnastic mat. After each diving roll, we would invite a member of the audience to join the girls kneeling down, and this would add up until I was diving over twelve people. One particular night, as members of the audience were joining the girls kneeling down, instead of kneeling on my side of the girls, they kept joining the side where the gymnastic mat was, which meant that, when there were about nine or ten persons in the group, the gymnastic mat was completely covered and I was landing on the hard wooden floor. I didn't have the nerve to point out the problem and went on to dive over the usual twelve. I certainly made sure that this never happened again.

We used to make our show as professional as possible and even had our own musical director, Johnnie Brown, a Cornish man, living in Letterston at the time, to provide our background music. All our shows were always well attended and seemed to be much appreciated by the audience. I know that we certainly enjoyed putting them on, and it went a little way towards fulfilling my dream, even if I wasn't getting paid.

One day in May 1949, a very good friend of mine, Ernest Davies, was home on leave from the Merchant Navy. At the time he was an apprentice on Anglo Saxon Oil Tankers. He later rose to the rank of Master Mariner and is today Director of a large marine salvage company in South Africa.

At that time, there was a big May fair at Haverfordwest. It was certainly the biggest fair that had been held in the county since before the war, and was attracting large crowds. We decided that we would go to the fair that evening to celebrate Ernie being home. As we were leaving the house to catch the bus, my father said to me, 'Mind that you keep away from that booth. You don't want to go to Aberdare on Saturday with a black eye.' My reply was 'What booth?' as honestly, I did not know what he was talking about. To put you in the picture, he was referring to a boxing booth which was at the fair for the first time in my days, and the 'Aberdare' bit was the fact that I was competing in the Welsh Weight-lifting Championships at Aberdare the following Saturday. As we left the house, I thought no more about what he had said.

When we arrived at the fair, it was massive and nothing like I had ever seen before. It was held in a big open area of the town called The Green, and the surrounding streets. We had

14

hardly pushed our way 50 yards through the crowds, when I heard a man's voice shouting, 'Come on, come on! I'll give 30 shillings (£1.50) to anyone who goes three rounds with Gunner Smith!'

On looking through the crowd, I could see what was the beautifully-painted front of the boxing booth, with about six or seven boxers lined up on the platform in front. The sight really impressed me and I started pushing my way further through the crowd to get a better view.

As I went forward, I could see that the voice I had heard was coming from a dapper little man standing in the middle of the platform with a microphone in his hand and, as I got nearer, he was repeating the challenge.

All I could hear ringing in my ears was 'thirty shillings'. Believe me, in those days, that was a lot of money. At that time, I was getting five shillings a week and my keep.

Before the little man had finished his challenge, I was shouting, 'I'll take him on.' Ernie, who was at my elbow, nearly died and hastened to remind me of what my father had said, but his words fell on deaf ears. Determined not to miss the chance, I continued to push my way forward until I was standing right beneath the man with the microphone. The fact that Gunner Smith, who he was referring to at the time, weighed probably a good three stones heavier than me, didn't register. The little man, who was the proprietor of the boxing booth, looked down at me and said, 'Go around the back, and you can borrow some shorts and gym shoes.'

Ernie, bless him, was still with me, and as I made my way around to the back of the booth, he was vehemently voicing what he thought of my 'bloody stupid idea. 'In the wagon behind the boxing booth, I accepted the offer of the gym shoes, but declined the shorts as I had skinny legs. Eventually, when it came to my turn to enter the ring, Ernie, being the friend he was, agreed to be in my corner. I had stripped off to the waist and had tucked my trousers inside my socks.

Although I say so myself, I knew that there was no-one fitter than me. With all my weight-lifting and balancing, I was as hard

15

as nails. The only fact that remained was, that I had never seen a boxing ring in my life, let alone been in one.

There was a loud cheer as I climbed into the ring. The booth was packed to capacity and I could see several people in the crowd that I knew. Looking across the ring to where my opponent was in the other corner, I could see that he was a lot bigger than me, but that didn't deter me in any way. The booth proprietor with his microphone, from the middle of the ring introduced us both and said that I had accepted the challenge, and would get 30 shillings if I went the three rounds. He then left the ring and another man climbed in to act as referee.

The bell sounded and Gunner Smith never left his corner. But, to be fair, that was no fault of his.

Before the bell had finished ringing, I was across the ring like a flash and must have hit him half a dozen times before he knew the fight had started. He never stood a chance, and went sprawling out through the ropes into the crowd. Several people in the crowd helped to push him back into the ring. He was just about back in the ring, when I hit him flush on the chin with a right hander. He somersaulted back in to the crowd and I never saw him again.

At first, the booth proprietor refused to pay me, saying that I had not gone the three rounds.

This caused pandemonium in the crowd and eventually, he paid me the 30 shillings. I left the booth feeling a rich man.

We enjoyed the rest of the evening at the fair, even though we had to walk home the 15 miles, having missed the last bus. I suffered during the walk home, as I was wearing a nearly new pair of brogue shoes, but still had to be in work by 8am. The word 'excuses' didn't figure in my father's book.

Boxing had always appealed to me, but probably the reason why I had never done any was because there were no boxing clubs near to where I lived. The nearest boxing club was at a place called Merlin's Bridge, about 17 miles from my home. I used to listen often to any fight that was on the radio. We had no television in those days, so the only boxing that I had seen was occasionally in the cinema. When the winter fairs came

16

around that year, and I knew that the boxing booth would be at Haverfordwest Fair on 5th October, I thought that it would be another opportunity for me to see how deep my interest really was in boxing, and also a chance to make a bit of extra money.

We organised a coach load from the youth club to go to the fair that year and Sybil came with us, although she was not a member of the youth club. As I said, I intended having another go in the boxing booth and this time brought a bit of kit with me, a pair of gym shoes and some shorts. When we arrived at the fair, we arranged for Sybil and the other girls to go and enjoy themselves; my mates and I would join them later. I told Sybil that I would meet her by the Wall of Death at about 9pm. My mates and I then went off to find the boxing booth.

When we got to the booth, I discovered that they had no-one near my weight, (9st 10lbs.).

The nearest they had was a lad called Joe Rogers, who was about 11st. I thought, nothing ventured nothing gained, so I decided to take him on. The previous night had been very windy with heavy rain, so the fairground people had taken the tilt (canvas roof) off the top of the booth to prevent any damage. Obviously, because of the heavy rain, the floor of the boxing ring had got very wet, so they had scattered sawdust on the floor to soak up the water.

Although Joe was big and strong, I was far too fast and fit for him and he took a tremendous amount of punishment. By the end of the three rounds, his face was covered with blood and sawdust, after the number of times that he had been knocked down. I hadn't realised how late it was. When Joe and I walked out of the booth, Sybil and her friends were waiting outside. Sybil saw Joe first and she nearly died. When I walked out behind Joe and she saw that there wasn't a mark on me, I could see the relief on her face.

There was no doubt in my mind now. I knew that I had caught the boxing bug, and on the 4th November 1949, I joined Merlin's Bridge Boxing Club. Three nights a week, I would make the 34 miles round journey on my bicycle for a couple of hours' training, no matter what the weather was. The star at

Merlin's Bridge Boxing Club in those days was a lad from Milford Haven, called Ronnie Atkins. Ronnie had a brilliant amateur record, but did not enjoy the same success when he turned professional some years later. I am pleased to say that Ronnie and I are still good pals today.

I had my first amateur fight at the Market Hall, Pembroke Dock, in February 1950: I won by a knock-out in the second round. It was the first time that I had ever been to Pembroke Dock and I did not see much of it then, as it was dark when we arrived. Little did I know then that one day I would be living there as a policeman and that my youngest daughter would be born there, but that's running away with my story.

My second amateur fight was at Amanford. I lost on points and broke the thumb of my left hand, which made me forget boxing for a while. When my thumb was better and I had the urge to fight again, I had two more amateur fights, one in Trecwn, which I lost on points, and my last one at the Market Hall, Haverfordwest, which I won by a knock-out in the second round. That was my total record as an amateur boxer. It had already started me thinking that if I could get knocked around for nothing, surely it made sense that I should get paid for it.

I had my first paid fight, apart from the boxing booth, when I topped the bill at an unlicensed show (which means that it was not under the auspices of the British Boxing Board of Control) at the Market Hall, Cardigan, against Eddie Stevens of Cardiff. I won by a knock-out in the second round.

When the winter fairs came around again in October 1951, Sybil and I went to Whitland Fair on our motor cycle, with my intention of boxing on the boxing booth again to make a bit of money. Whitland was the first fair of the season down the West Wales area. When we arrived at the fairground and I spoke to the proprietor of the booth, he told me that he did not have any boxers of my weight. He said that the nearest he had was a professional middleweight called Wyndam Alexander. I said that I did not mind the weight difference and that I would take him on, after being told that I would get £1 for every round I went. It may be hard to understand these days, but then, £1 was a lot of money. Despite the weight difference, I easily went the three rounds and came away with £3, which made the trip worthwhile.

Before I left the booth, the proprietor, Ron Taylor, recognised me as the boy who had beaten a couple of his boxers before, and he asked me if I was interested in boxing for him on the booth. I gladly accepted. For the next six years, I boxed on the booth at all the fairgrounds in Wales, starting in Neath, down through Carmarthenshire, Pembrokeshire, Cardiganshire and ending up in Aberystwyth. Incidentally, Ron and his wife Lily became very good friends of Sybil and myself and are still so today. A couple of years ago, we went to Ron's 80th birthday in Gloucester and he looked no different than the first time I met him. He's a great bloke.

I have many good memories of my days boxing on the fairground booth, but there was one night which I could well have done without. It was a Saturday night of Pembroke Fair week.

I was boxing a young challenger from the crowd and had forgotten to bring my gumshield with me. I don't wish to sound big-headed, but it was my intention to let him go the three rounds. We did this sometimes, if there were not many bouts on, and to encourage challengers to take part. In the first round, I got caught with a punch on the mouth. It was not an exceptionally hard punch, and I thought nothing of it, except that I could taste blood in my mouth and that was not unusual. At the end of the round, I went back to my corner, and my second, who was Jimmy Taylor, Ron's brother, asked me to open my mouth for him to see.

I did this and when I saw the look on his face, I knew that there was something really wrong.

Jimmy said that he was stopping the fight there and then, but I pleaded with him to let me have one more minute, probably because I had never been beaten on the boxing booth and did not want to lose that record. Very reluctantly, he said, 'Right, one minute only.' By now, my mouth was feeling very strange and was filling up with blood. When the bell sounded for the second round, I wanted to get the fight over with quickly and I

19

knocked the challenger out with first punch. I could now feel the blood coming out of my mouth like a tap and I knew that it was not just a nick on my tongue. They immediately took me up to the cottage hospital, which was next to the police station and only about 100 yards from the boxing booth.

The duty nurse, when she saw my tongue, nearly fainted, and it was only then that I saw it for the first time in a mirror and it gave me quite a shock. The tongue was split completely in half, right down the middle,(as the Indians would say, 'Man with forked tongue.) There was no resident doctor at the hospital, but one arrived in a short time. I don't remember how many stitches they put in my tongue, but by the time they had finished, the swelling was such that I could hardly breath. The doctor said that I would have to be kept in for the night, so that they could keep an eye on me.

Needless to say, I didn't sleep a wink all night. Many times I have thought since, if only I'd known then, that one day I would be living at the police station next door. One never knows, do they? Next morning, after the doctor had seen me, I was discharged and I went down to where the boys were dismantling the booth, ready to go on to Letterston Fair for the next week. I obviously couldn't eat any dinner, as good as it smelled. Ron's wife Lily had cooked a lovely roast rabbit dinner, but I had to content myself with the juice of two tins of fruit which Lily had opened for me. I could only drink this through a straw.

When we arrived in Letterston on the Sunday evening, Ron drove me home to Goodwick in his car. I wasn't married then, but still living at home with my mum and dad. They were not at home, having gone to church, so I went up to Sybil's house and found that she was in chapel.

Before going down to meet her, I had to write a note explaining exactly what had happened, as by now, my tongue was so swollen, that I couldn't speak a word. Later that evening, the swelling got even worse and we had to call the doctor to give me injections. Naturally, I thought that I would be out of action for months, but just over two weeks later, I was boxing at Cardigan Fair.

CHAPTER THREE
BOXING PROFESSIONALLY

In the meantime I had applied to the British Boxing Board of Control for a professional boxer's licence, which I was granted without a trial fight and although I had had only four amateur bouts. I had my first official professional fight at the Market Hall, Carmarthen, on 14th April 1952, when I beat a welterweight, Harold Urch, over six rounds.

Because there were no boxing clubs near where I lived, I obviously had to rely very much on the winter fairs, when I could get plenty of ring practice in the boxing booth. I learned a lot from boxing with Al Brown from British Guiana, who was travelling with the booth at that time. Also, because of where I lived, I did not have a boxing manager, which made it very difficult for me to get fights and to get myself known, although I had won my first fight.

One night, when I was boxing on the booth at Neath Fair, I met a boxing manager by the name of Tommy Dunn from Chester. He was a real gentleman. I explained to him the difficulty I was experiencing in getting fights and asked him if he could help me in any way. He had, of course, seen me boxing many times on the booth and said that he would do what he could to get me matched up somewhere in the Midlands.

I found Mr Dunn to be very much a man of his word: a few weeks later I had a letter from him telling me that he had managed to get me a contest fighting Norman Wormall, chief supporting bout at Walsall Town Hall, on 10th December 1952. Professional boxing in those days at Walsall Town Hall was always on a Monday night, so that meant that I would have to catch the mail train out of Fishguard on the Sunday evening and travel overnight to Birmingham and then on to Walsall.

On the Saturday morning, two days before the fight, I woke up sweating and shivering like mad and realised that I had a bad bout of the flu. I was in bed all day Saturday and Sunday morning. I was not married then and still living at home with my mum and dad. Of course, Sybil was at the house on the Saturday and Sunday, and they were all telling me that I could forget about going to Walsall. Although I could hardly stand, I kept thinking of all the pleading that I had made to Tommy Dunn, and now here I was, with the likelihood of me not turning up for the fight. The more I thought about it, the more determined I was, that there was no way that I was going to let him down.

Ignoring all the pleas from Sybil and my parents, and I admit probably foolishly, I caught the train at 6.20 that Sunday evening and after travelling through the night, arrived at Birmingham about 5.30am on the Monday to find the ground covered with about 2 inches of snow. I caught a bus up to Walsall and, at the expense of showing what a fool I was, walked around Walsall all day, because I did not know that there was a 1pm weigh-in. I did not even have a cup of tea all day in case I weighed-in overweight and had to pay a forfeit. Incidentally, my purse money for the fight was £10, and that was before I paid my expenses.

It probably goes without saying that, I lost the fight, getting stopped in the fourth round. I have thought many times since, how the hell did I go four rounds? Although very disappointed with the outcome of things, I am sure that the whole experience made me more determined than ever to show people that I could do a lot better. I got back home, went back to work for my dad and settled down to plenty of road work and bag punching. Right through my boxing career, I used to run about 12 miles every day, no matter what the weather, or what day it was.

The following March, I had my next fight at the Market Hall, Haverfordwest, when I boxed a welter-weight, Terry Bannon, from Merthyr and beat him on points over six rounds. Actually, I boxed five or six welter-weights during my career, although I was a natural light-weight.

Just over a week later, I was grossly over-matched, fighting another welter-weight, Sandy Manuel of Nigeria, in the chief supporting bout at Willenhall Baths. I took the fight with less than 24 hours notice, because his original opponent had been injured. I lost the fight in the second round, being stopped with a punch that was well below the belt. I am not suggesting for

22

one moment that the foul was deliberate; there was no need for it to be, he was far too experienced for me.

On the 4th November 1953, the boxing promoter, Johnny Best, booked me for a six round contest against Wally Barkas from Bolton at Liverpool Stadium. This was a very famous boxing venue, and I was thrilled to be boxing there so soon in my career. Because the purse money for the fight was only £10, and to save money, I decided to travel to Liverpool on my motor-cycle, which was a Douglas Horizontal Speed Twin. What I did not know then was that the Douglas motor-cycles were made in Kingswood, Bristol, a few hundred yards away from where I would be living many years later.

A very good friend of mine, Norman Duggan, came to Liverpool with me to share the driving.

Of course, at that time, I did not have a boxing manager and had to rely on whoever was available at the venue to look after me in my corner. Although Wally Barkas had come into professional boxing after a long amateur career, he gave me no trouble really, and I won by a knock-out in the second round. On the return journey from Liverpool that night, we drove most of the way home through blinding rain, but I don't think that Norman nor I noticed it, as we were still on a high after me winning the fight. I'm sure that Norman didn't stop talking about it for weeks.

My next fight caused quite a stir in the boxing world. In late November 1953, I was matched against Billy Cobb from Chesterfield at Derby, in a fight that was to make headlines in the National Press. I was the first boxer, under a new rule made by the British Boxing Board of Control, to be left lying unconscious on the floor of the ring for the whole minute interval without receiving medical attention. Just before the bell sounded to end the third round of the fight, I was caught by a punch which knocked me to the floor. As I fell, my head struck the floor of the ring and I was rendered unconscious. Under the new rule, my cornerman removed my gumshield from my mouth and then had to leave me unattended until the bell sounded for the start of the fourth round. The next day, Peter Wilson, the

23

well known *Daily Mirror* Sports Journalist, wrote a scathing report, pointing out what a ridiculous and dangerous rule it was. It meant that a boxer could be bleeding to death, and yet had to be left without any medical attention for the full minute. Fortunately, the British Boxing Board of Control saw the danger of the rule and it was changed.

Being so far away from professional boxing circles, meant that it was extremely difficult for me to get myself known, so that I could get regular fights. As I did not have a manager, I realised that I would have to do something about this or pack it all in. I had received a few offers from London managers, who insisted however, on the condition that I would have to live in London. This, obviously, was not what I wanted, but which left me for the time being undecided.

Towards the end of 1953, I signed up under the management of Bill Dixie of Crewe, who was also a British Boxing Board of Control Matchmaker.

In early January 1954, *Boxing News* announced that the National Sporting Club in London was staging a professional light-weight competition, and that 'Boxing News' would be awarding the winner a gold watch; he would also become the protégé of the National Sporting Club. My manager, Bill Dixie, wrote to me saying that he had entered me for the competition and, although I was always 100% fit, I got down to even harder training as a result of this good news. I did most of my training for the competition in the motor-cycle workshop of my friend, Roy Williams. With all the motor-cycles, etc. in the workshop, there was hardly room to swing a cat, but then, beggers can't be choosers.

I was informed that the first series of the competition was to be at the National Sporting Club on 15th February. One bad bit of news that I had was that my manager, Bill Dixie, was ill in bed with pleurisy and that I would have to travel to London on my own. As it was, I travelled to London on the night of 14th February, booking a sleeper on the overnight train to Paddington. It was a bit of a waste of money really, as I didn't sleep a wink all night but, at least, I was lying down, and that was something.

When I arrived at the National Sporting Club for the 1pm weigh-in, I discovered that my pal Ronnie Atkins, from Milford Haven, was also in the competition, and his dad was with him as his trainer. It gave me a little comfort, knowing that there were friends there from near home. In the first series of the competition, I was drawn against Colin Staples of Doncaster.

I weighed-in at 9st.10lbs., and knocked him out in the second round with a left hook, which was my favourite punch.

They decided to hold the second series of the competition the same evening, and I was drawn against Bob Murray, a Scots blacksmith, who had beaten Ronnie Atkins on points in the first series. Ron's father came in my corner for the fight and, although I found Murray a hard nut to crack, I beat him on points, which took me into the final against Len Wilson from Dagenham, who was unbeaten as a professional. In my second fight, I hadn't got off scot free, as I had taken a hard punch on my right cheek and had a suspect fracture of the upper jaw bone, The right side of my face was badly swollen and my right eye discoloured.

When I arrived home on the early morning train next day, Sybil was at the railway station meeting me. When she saw my face, she turned white, and I hastened to tell her that I had won both my fights and was in the final. When she realised that I was OK, she was not so worried.

I went to the hospital for an X-ray on my face and fortunately I did not have a fracture, but very bad bruising.

The final of the competition had been fixed for 1st March, St David's Day, which gave me less than two weeks to get fit. I got in touch with my manager and told him about my damaged cheek bone and, although he was still ill, he said that he would get in touch with London and try to get the final postponed until my face was better. He soon got back in touch with me and said that they had refused to postpone the final, and that if I did not turn up, I would forfeit the fight. Believe me, this was bad news for the London Camp, as it made me more determined than ever.

On the night of 29th February, I again booked an overnight sleeper to Paddington, knowing that once again I was on my own. At the National Sporting Club the next day, I weighed-in at 1pm and was exactly 9st 8lbs. I knew that I was in the pink of condition, but something else I knew was that Len Wilson was a very classy boxer and that I would not be able to outbox him. As I was walking down the aisle towards the ring that night, Dick Turpin, brother of the great Randolph Turpin, shouted to me, 'Fight him your usual way Bryn, and he won't last.'

Dick, at that time, was a boxing manager and one of his fighters, Andy Baird, was on the same bill. Andy, incidentally, had lost on points to Len Wilson in the second series of the competition.

As the bell rang for the start of the first round, I remembered some advice I had been given some years before, 'Let the opposition think that you are a little greener than what you really are.' In that first round, although I was looking after myself, I let him catch me with some punches that I really could have avoided. Whilst this probably gave him some confidence, it also had the desired effect of making him a little cocky.

The *Boxing News* write-up, said of the first round, 'Wilson, cutting out all the frills, was using the ring well, and sneaking the points with short crisp punches to head and body.' They said of the second round, 'Then quite suddenly, came disaster for the young Dagenham clerk. He stood his ground against one of Phillips' rushes and tried to pull up his man short with a right hander. But, in attempting this rather commendable stroke, Wilson made the mistake of leaving his chin unguarded. The Londoner never saw the right-hander that crashed on to his chin. He dropped to the canvas in a heap and only just recovered to stand erect at the count of eight, although badly shaken.'

'Wilson managed to take a couple of strides across the ring and get his back to the ropes, but Phillips was on him like a flash, and before the dazed Londoner could attempt to raise his guard, Phillips brought up a left hook to the open target of Wilson's chin and Len was on the canvas again. Gamely, he tried to throw off the effects of the punch, but in vain. He stood erect once more at eight, but his knees would not support his spirit, and Referee, George Carney, wisely stopped the bout.'

On behalf of Mr Vivian Brodsky, proprietor of *Boxing News*, Len Harvey, former undefeated British and Empire Heavyweight Champion, presented me with the *Boxing News* gold watch.

In a short speech to the members, Len Harvey said, 'I had no idea that such good boxing went on at this club. I thought you had to go to places like Earls Court or Harringay to see a good fight.' He went on to say, 'I'm glad to see many familiar faces around the ringside and it is good to know that there are still a few Corinthians left in the game.'

I felt so proud standing there in the middle of the ring, especially as it was St David's Day.

The only disappointment I felt was that there was no-one there from home to share my brief moment of glory.

That disappointment vanished the next morning when I arrived home and Sybil was once again at the railway station to greet me. The look on her face when I showed her the gold watch meant more to me than anything the night before. I knew that I had won it for her, because she supported everything I did.

Two weeks later, I was matched to fight Peter Hill of Leyton, top of the bill at the National Sporting Club. They were in fact keeping to their promise of making me their protégé and giving me regular engagements in London.

Once again I travelled to London on the overnight train, as I was never one to leave things to the last minute. It meant that I would arrive in plenty of time for the weigh-in and then rest up for the afternoon. It was only when I was actually in the ring that evening and we were being introduced to the crowd by the MC that I knew that my opponent was not to be Peter Hill, but Pat McCoy, a much more experienced fighter. McCoy was a short, rugged fighter who came forward all the time, throwing punches from all angles. No-one had had the decency to tell

27

me of the change of opponent, not that it would have made any difference. I would still have gone ahead with the fight.

As I said, McCoy was very short for a light-weight and I kept catching him on the top of his head with my left leads. It was in the second round that I caught him with a good solid left and actually felt the bone snapping in my left hand as I hit him. It was near the end of the round and because of the pain, it was my intention to retire in the interval to prevent further damage.

As I sat in the corner, being tended to by my second who was a stranger, because my manager was still ill, I thought, 'What would they think of me, if I was to quit now?' and like a fool, I decided to carry on. I tried for the rest of the fight to use my left hand as little as possible, but against an opponent like Pat McCoy, that was asking the impossible. You simply had to use both hands all time, if only to prevent him smothering you with punches. The fight ended in a draw and, although I was disappointed, I thought that it was better than losing.

When they took off my gloves and bandages, my left hand looked grotesque. It was badly swollen and I couldn't close it. I travelled home on the overnight train feeling pretty much down in the dumps. I went to the hospital soon after I arrived home, had the hand X-rayed and was put in plaster. I was told that I had broken the second meta-carpal and that I should give it at least six weeks before I boxed again. Obviously, I should have retired as soon as I felt the hand break. Although I was not to know it then, this break to my hand was to bug me for the rest of my career, I took the advice that I had been given and did not box again until 22nd July, when I was matched against Del Willis, a Jamaican, at Liverpool Stadium. Willis was a bustling type of fighter who lead with his head, although not intentionally. I felt my left hand go again in the first round. In the second round, Willis was disqualified for persistent use of his head. He was not a dirty fighter, it was just his style.

Again to save on expenses, I had travelled to Liverpool on my motor-cycle, a Sunbeam shaft-drive which I had then. As one knows, in order to change gear you have to de-clutch by using the clutch lever on the left handlebar and, on the Sunbeam,

28

it took quite some strength to use the lever. You can imagine the pain I felt all the way home, every time I changed gear. When I arrived home and took off my thick motor-cycle gloves, the broken bone was sticking out through the skin on the back of my left hand. That meant another repair job and a long lay-off.

In the October issue of the American boxing magazine, 'The Ring', I was rated the best light-weight prospect of the month. I was the only British boxer in the ratings.

Again, I had a very long lay-off to give my hand plenty of time to heal. It was in plaster until the middle of September, when I again started light training. Of course, I was doing road-work even when my hand was in plaster; there was no way that I was going to lose the condition I had built myself up to over the years. Obviously, there's a difference between fit and fighting fit.

Fighting fit is the condition you get yourself into a couple of weeks before a fight.

My next fight was against Teddy Best of Cardiff at the Market Hall, Carmarthen, on 25th October 1954. Many thought again that I was being badly overmatched, as Teddy was a very experienced fighter with a good amateur record before he turned professional. He also had a good professional record and had had many more fights than me. I knew that if my hand held out, I would be able to hold my own against him. As it was, I was beaten on points over eight rounds, after again breaking my left hand in the third round. The result surprised many, and apart from breaking my hand again, I was very pleased with my performance.

Sitting at ringside that night was a very good friend of mine, Billy Hall, a Fishguard businessman and one of my most ardent fans. Billy came to see me in my dressing room after the fight, and was genuinely pleased with my performance. He readily admitted that he thought that I had been overmatched, as he had seen Teddy Best box many times and knew how good he was. Billy had a friend of his with him and introduced him to me as Len Davies, a Canadian ex-boxer. Len kept a pub, the Dinas Arms, in Lower Fishguard. When Len asked me where I trained and I told him that most of my training was road-work and some bag punching, and that I only got some sparring for a couple of months in the winter, when the boxing booth came to the winter fairs, he could hardly believe me. He told me that if I was interested, he would be willing to take over my training and to have a think about it. I immediately told him that it didn't need any thinking and that I would be delighted to take up his offer. The result was that he made me a gym in one of the back rooms of the pub and I trained there up to the time when I finished boxing. That was a long time ago, and I believe that the pub is no longer there, but I still have a memory jolt everytime I pass there in the car.

All the time that I trained at the Dinas Arms, I had another good friend who lived near the pub and used to help me with my training. His name is Davy Griffiths. Davy wouldn't hear a bad word about me and thought that I was capable of beating anyone in the world. He used to even spar with me. Whenever I lost a fight, I always felt as if I'd let Davy down.

In the January 1955 issue of *Boxing News*, I was upgraded to a three star light-weight.

One evening at the beginning of March 1955, Sybil and I were up at my mum and dad's house visiting. My dad and I were watching boxing on the television. Sybil and I couldn't afford one.

There was a fight on from Liverpool Stadium, Bobby Gill, a Jamaican welter-weight was boxing Trevor Sykes from Huddersfield. As it was, the fight ended in a draw, but my dad was of the opinion that black boxers should not fight white ones, because the black boxers were tougher, and he thought that it was not fair. I, of course, disagreed with him and told him that was a load of rubbish, but it wouldn't change his views and we left it at that.

On the 10th March, I travelled to Liverpool as my manager, Bill Dixie, had said that Johnny Best, the promoter at Liverpool Stadium, had promised to get me a fight on the bill. When we arrived at the Stadium it turned out that Johnny Best had failed to get me an opponent. He could see how disappointed I was

Bryn Phillips -vs- Teddy Best

31

Bryn being presented with a gold watch by Len Harvey
at the National Sporting Club, London on 1st March 1954

after coming all that way, and said that he would definitely put me on as chief supporting contest at Blackpool Tower Circus the following night, where he was also the promoter. I was obviously delighted with the news and telephoned home to let them know that I would be staying the night with my manager at Crewe, and that I would be boxing at Blackpool the following night, but that I did not know who my opponent was.

Next day, we arrived at Blackpool Tower about 12 noon. We went to the Tower Circus office to find out who I would be boxing that evening. They were busy there, erecting the ring and overhead lights. Johnny Best had not yet arrived but his clerk was in the office. He told us that the programmes had not yet been printed but he had a list of the fights for that night. Looking at the list, he said that I would be boxing a Bobby Gill of Jamaica. My manager said, 'He can't be, he's a welter-weight. ' Well, that's what is on the list', the clerk said. I looked at Dixie, as he was affectionately know, and said, 'Never mind the weight difference, I'm not going home without a fight now. 'Actually, at the weigh-in, I was 9st 10lbs. and Bobby Gill scaled exactly 10st. so the weight difference was not too bad.

When I entered the ring that night, in the packed out arena, I was so determined to do well, remembering what my dad had said about black boxers. I thought, if only he could see me now.

The fight lasted less than one round. The write-up in *Boxing News* the following week was. 'BRYN PHILLIPS IN PUNCHING SPREE AGAINST GILL. Phillips tore into his man right from the first bell and, after parrying him with neat lefts, rocked him with a beautiful right hook flush to the jaw. Gill took the punch without falling and he back-peddled in his attempt to avoid the follow-up, but he was not quick enough to escape Phillips' next blow, a hard left hook to the solar plexus, and Gill took every pound of it, as he fell against the middle rope. Phillips backed away, waiting for his man to hit the deck, but Gill regained his stance without going down. Phillips again advanced and another left hook, this time to the jaw, put the Jamaican boy down, where he stayed for a nine count. Gill was still feeling the effects of the first body punch and he had little to offer in defence except a weak sort of left jab, and another left to the side of the head sent him down for a further count, this time for 'eight. 'This was the beginning of the end for Gill, but he would not give in and again squared up as his man came forward for a third time. Phillips first measured him with a short left and then whipped over a sickening hard right hook to the jaw which lifted Gill clean off his feet. He scrambled to his feet at the count of 'nine', but was in no fit state to continue, and the referee wisely intervened to save him from further punishment'.

Again, thinking of what my dad had said about black boxers, as soon as I left the ring and still in my dressing gown, I rushed to the nearest telephone to let them know at home how I had got on. I knew that Sybil would be up at my parents and would be waiting for news. At that time my mum and dad did not have a telephone at the house but only in the office at the nursery about half a mile away. I also knew that my dad would be at the nursery that time, banking the furnaces down for the night. Although I did not know it then, there was a funny sequel to my telephone call that night. When my dad heard the telephone ringing, he was in one of the boiler houses throwing coal into the furnace. He had my youngest brother Gwyn with him in the boiler house. When he rushed out to answer the telephone, because it was late and dark, he told Gwyn to stay in the boiler house and then bolted the door from the outside. When my dad had my call on the telephone, he was so excited that he ran all the way home to tell Sybil and my mum, and it was only after he had told them the news that he remembered about Gwyn in the locked boiler house.

My next fight was a chief supporting contest at Liverpool Stadium, on 14th April 1955, when I was stopped in the fifth. round by Leo Molloy of Birkenhead. I'm not making any excuses, because Leo was an extremely good fighter and, although I did not break my hand on this occasion, the previous breaks were beginning to have a psychological effect on my boxing and my training. It was getting to the state when I was afraid to use my left hand.

34

This was discussed the next time I saw the orthopaedic specialist, who informed me that the bone, after all the breaks, was now in such condition that the only answer was to have a bone graft.

On 18th May 1955, I was admitted to the Orthopaedic Ward, in Glangwilli Hospital, Carmarthen, to have the bone graft that the specialist had recommended. The orthopaedic surgeon, Mr Mervyn Evans, took a piece of bone out from the right side of my pelvis and, after shaping it, grafted it as a new second metacarpal into my left hand. In all, the bone had broken in five different fights.

In the 17th June 1955 issue of *Boxing News*, they wrote,' 'GOOD NEWS OF PHILLIPS, Nice to hear that Bryn Phillips, the Fishguard light-weight, who won a *Boxing News* gold watch last year, is now out of hospital after an operation to his left hand. He is making good progress and hopes to be back in action by the end of the year. A famous West Wales surgeon took a piece of bone out from Bryn's hip and grafted it into his left hand. Incidentally, Bryn is a highly skilled gymnast and handbalancer. He is a very keen physical-culturist and a conscientious worker in the gym. He is now doing a lot of gripping exercises, in order to strengthen his hands. But Bryn lacks sparring partners and has to rely on local boys at his youth club.'

For a long time after the operation I had very serious doubts about carrying on boxing and it was over six months before I cast aside those doubts and accepted another chief supporting bout at the Winter Gardens, Malvern, where on the 28th November 1955, I boxed Johnny King of Birmingham and beat him on points over six rounds. I had no trouble with my left hand; obviously this did much to restore a little of my confidence.

After another winter season on the boxing booth, I was booked to fight Pat McCoy in an eight round contest on the Dai Dower bill, at the Market Hall, Carmarthen, on the 30th January, 1956. At that time, Pat was receiving a lot of publicity in the national press, as he had been sparring partner to Dai

Dower. Many locals thought that I was being badly overmatched again. They did not know that I had boxed him before in London. You see, in those days, I didn't have any publicity or write-ups in the local press, only in the *Boxing News*, which the general public did not see.

Before the fight, I'd been given instructions by my trainer, Len Davies, to box McCoy and keep out of trouble. I did not agree with these tactics but, as always, did as I was told. I had two coach loads of supporters in the crowd that night, including our local vicar from home, my dad and my youngest brother Gwyn. For the first three rounds, I stuck to my instructions and took a hell of a hiding. In my heart, I knew that you couldn't box a fighter like Pat McCoy, nor could you keep out of trouble because of his style. He was the type of fighter who climbed all over you, throwing punches from all angles and non-stop. At the end of the third round I went back to my corner, sat on the stool, and said to Len, 'That's the bloody end of that. 'Len looked startled and said. 'You are not packing in are you?' and I replied, ' No, bloody starting.'

For the next five rounds I showed Pat that I could also play it rough and throw punches non- stop from all angles. The fight ended in a draw, which, after my first pathetic three rounds, wasn't a bad verdict for me. But I still felt in my heart that I had the beating of him and knew that if I met him again, I was going to fight under my rules.

Well, it wasn't very long before that chance materialised. On 7th July that same year, we met again at an open air show in Aberystwyth, over eight rounds. This time, I had no intention of trying to box him and to be fair to Len, he did not suggest it either. I had decided, even after my first meeting with Pat, that the only way to beat him was to play him at his own game.

This time I showed him that I could do that as well as him. From the first bell there were no quarters asked and certainly none given. It was voted as the best fight of the night in the press and it was described by the old time fighter Jimmy Wild as, 'One man with two pairs of hands giving himself a heck of a hiding. 'I won the fight on points and was delighted because

Sybil was there watching. It was the only official professional fight that she had ever come to watch me and, believe me, she couldn't have picked a rougher one. Although I did not break my hand in the fight, I badly damaged it, which again put doubts in my mind about carrying on.

Probably time helped the doubts to disappear and for 23rd October 1956, I was booked for another chief-supporting bout at Willenhall Baths, against Andy Baird of Birmingham. I can honestly say that it was one of the worse days of my life. For all my sins, I have always been a very punctual guy and can't stand being late for anything.

At that time, my trainer, Len Davies, as well as keeping a pub, worked for a frozen food company and delivered the goods in a Bedford van that had sliding doors and frozen food containers in the back, which, even when empty, gave off a horrible smell. I had suggested to Len that I should travel to Willenhall on the train the day before the fight and he could follow up in the van on the day of the fight. He wouldn't hear of it and insisted that we both travel up together in the van on the day of the fight. He said that it would save money and, like a fool I agreed. He did tell me that on the day of the fight, he would not be working and we could make an early start. He said that he would pick me up at the house at 8 o'clock in the morning.

Well, being me, I was ready to go at 7 o'clock. 8 o'clock came, 8.15, 8.30, 8.45, and no sign of Len. Just before 9 o'clock, he arrived, as if we had all day to get there. By now I was feeling really on edge but believe me that was only the beginning.

We left Goodwick and drove up into Fishguard with hardly a word spoken. When we approached Fishguard Square, I expected him to turn left towards Cardigan which, in those days without the benefit of todays motorways, would have been the best and quickest way to get to Willenhall in time for the 1pm weigh-in. At the Square, he turned right towards Haverfordwest. I did not say anything, because I honestly thought he was pulling my leg.

37

When I saw that he was carrying on, I asked him why we were going that way, and it was then that he told me that he had some deliveries to make first in the south of the county.

I must admit, I was dumb-struck. For the next two hours we were travelling in completely the opposite direction to which we wanted to go. He made his last delivery in Freshwater East, a little seaside place, which many years later brought back the memory of that day, because it was one of the places I covered when I was a police sergeant in Pembroke. But, to get back to the story, at 1.10pm that day, we were sitting in a little cafe in a place called Narberth. That was 10 minutes after I should have weighed-in at Willenhall, and we were further away from Willenhall than we were when we started out.

I have never felt so demoralised in my life and, in despair, suggested that we telephoned Alex Griffiths, the promoter, and tell him a white lie that we had broken down and could not get there. This made me feel terrible as I had never ever let any promoter down, and had a reputation for it. Len said that we would get there in plenty of time, as we headed off north.

I don't know whether he'd forgotten that I had an eight-round fight ahead of me. The journey up was a nightmare; with van rocking and rolling and the terrible smell from the frozen food containers, I was actually physically sick and felt awful. We were passing through Wolverhampton just before 7pm and we stopped at a telephone box to ring the promoter, to tell him that we were nearly there. He wasn't very happy at the fact that I hadn't turned for the weigh-in, and I didn't blame him. When we arrived at the hall, I had to weigh-in immediately and, half an hour later, I was in the ring.

I suppose it goes without saying that I lost the fight. I survived a knock-down in the first round, had a badly cut eye in the second round, and lost the fight on points.

The headlines in the *Boxing News* the following week was, 'THEY LIKED BRYN'. The report went on to say that the applause of the crowd was well deserved for my 'never say die' attitude. That praise did nothing to make me feel any better, nor to erase my memories of that day. I have never been one to hold a grudge, but that fight was lost for me before I got there.

On the 12th November, 1956, I boxed Ronnie Rush of Trinidad at Cardiff, which was to be over eight rounds. Unfortunately, Ronnie was disqualified in the second round for a low punch.

Although I was disabled for a short while, I felt that the referee, after giving me time to recover, could have allowed the fight to continue, because it was obvious that the low punch had not been deliberate. On the 3rd December 1956, I topped the bill at the Hippodrome, Great Yarmouth, against Derek Clarke of Burnley. It was a time of the petrol rationing and the weigh-in was staged at Jack Soloman's Gym in Great Windmill Street, London. Then everyone was taken to Great Yarmouth by coach. At that time, I was managed by Dennis Granville, from Gloucester, as my first manager, Bill Dixic had died. Dennis had three other boxers from his stable on the same bill. I knew that Derek Clarke was a very experienced and busy boxer.

In fact, this was his 19th fight that year.

As I entered the ring that night, I thought, 'Catch him before he catches me', and that's exactly what I did. The *Boxing News* headlines the following week read, 'PHILLIPS CAPSIZES CLARKE.' As he moved in right at the start of the first round, I stepped inside his lead and caught him with a short right, which dropped him for the count of nine. In fact, I had him down five times in the first round. He came out for the second, and I was determined not to let him off the hook. I dropped him three times before referee Mickey Fox called a halt.

Once again, I had a good season on the boxing booth during the winter fairs, and on the 16th January 1957, I had my second encounter with Teddy Best of Cardiff, at the Sophia Gardens, Cardiff. The points verdict in favour of Best was not well received by his home crowd, nor by the press, who thought that I had edged it. I must admit that, whilst I take nothing away from Teddy, who was a good fighter, I really thought that I had done enough to win. Everyone I spoke to agreed, but it's the referee that counts. I went to Belfast for my next fight at the Ulster Hall, against Belfast southpaw, Sammy Cowan.

I don't wish for this to sound like excuse-making, but I'd travelled by train from Fishguard to Gloucester on the Friday. Soon after arriving at Gloucester, with my manager, Dennis Granville and three other boxers, we left by car for Liverpool. We left the car there and travelled by train to Heysham, where we caught the overnight ferry to Belfast.

To say that I was shattered when we arrived in Belfast would be an understatement. After the 1pm weigh-in, we just had to hang around, waiting for the evening. The fight was an eight round, chief supporting contest. In the second round of the fight, I had had two bad cuts on my left eye. The eyelid and the eyebrow were cut. Cowan was warned by the referee several times for leading with his head, but I didn't think that any of it was intentional. What did upset me was the fact that the referee stopped the fight in the seventh round in favour of Cowan because of my cut eye, which was no worse in the seventh round than it had been it the second.

Straight after the fight we had to rush by taxi, with me still dressing, to catch the ferry back to Heysham. It was early evening on Sunday when I arrived home.

On the 18th February 1957, I boxed another chief supporting contest at the Cafe Royal, London, losing on points to Barney Beale of Lambeth, over eight rounds. I next topped the bill at Wembley Town Hall, on 19th March , against Arthur Murphy of Camden Town. I received a very bad cut to my left eye in the third round and had to retire. At the beginning of May, 1957, I had a letter from the Welsh Area Council of the British Boxing Board of Control, informing me that I had been matched with Teddy Best of Cardiff on 27th May for the Welsh Light-weight Title.

Unfortunately, I was already contracted for a return fight with Arthur Murphy at Wembley on 16th May. There is a Boxing Board of Control rule which states that one cannot fight within 21 days of a title fight. The Welsh Area Council convened a special meeting and it was agreed that the title fight could go ahead, as long as I did not receive any injuries at the Wembley fight. As it turned out, I again received a very bad cut to my left eye in the second round of the Wembley fight on the 16th May, so my title fight had to be put on hold. It was very disappointing, because I was to have my biggest purse ever for that title fight. It also seemed that, having got over years of broken hand trouble, I was now being plagued with cut eye problems.

I retired from boxing in August 1957. At about 5.30am on 8th August, my first daughter, Marianne was born at home.

Just after 9am that morning, I had a telegram from my manager Dennis Granville, telling me that I was fighting Teddy Best of Cardiff for the Welsh Light-weight Title at Cross Keys on 21st August. Obviously, with our first baby having just been born, I did not think that I was in the right frame of mind to take such an important fight with such short notice. I thought that my priority for the next couple of weeks was to be home with my wife.

I immediately got on the telephone to my manager at Gloucester. I told him that Sybil had just had the baby and that I did not think that I should take the fight now, especially with such short notice. Just like all boxing managers, he went on about how hard he had worked to get me the title fight, and how I would be letting him down. Like a fool, I let him talk me into agreeing to take the fight. If only at the time I had let my heart rule my head. I should have insisted on the fight being put on hold until I was ready to do myself justice. I could not have been denied the title chance, because I was a leading contender in any case.

After talking it over with Sybil, I decided that I would go away to Gloucester to train, especially after Dennis had told me that there would be plenty of sparring partners there for me to train with. I caught the train to Gloucester the next morning and, on arriving at my manager's home, found that that there were no sparring partners at all, as they were all away on a boxing booth down Bournemouth way. I got down to my road work and bag-punching at Gloucester, but my mind all the time was at home with Sybil and the baby. In any case, I thought

41

that the training that I was doing, I could do just as well at home, so after two days in Gloucester, much against my manager's insistence, I went back home. In the meantime, Dennis had got on to the press, informing them that I had had over a hundred rounds of sparring with different fighters and that I was in the pink of condition. I agreed with the condition part, at least physically, but I'd had no sparring at all, and that was the most important part.

Back at home, I kept up the roadwork and bag punching as usual and I had a few rounds of sparring with my good friend, Billy James from Tegryn. On the day of the fight, I travelled to Cross Keys by car. To be absolutely honest, I was there physically but my mind was back at home.

During my training for the fight, I had pulled a muscle in my left thigh, when I was doing my roadwork. I had said nothing to anyone about it, as I was never one to make excuses and, in any case, it had not caused me too much bother. During the fight, probably due to the extra physical effort, I could feel the pain in my left thigh getting worse. It wasn't my style to take it easy in the ring and I always gave the crowd their money's-worth. By about the sixth round, the pain in my thigh was such that I could hardly put any weight on it, yet I was denying to my corner that there was anything wrong. In the ninth round, it was so painful that I was unable to move around the ring properly, and I was taking punches that I should be avoiding. At the end of the ninth round, although I was not taking too much punishment, I decided to call it a day and I retired. I called over the MC and asked him if he would thank the crowd on my behalf and announce that I was, as from then, retiring from boxing.

I don't know, maybe the problems that I'd had over the years had caught up with me, and in any case, I didn't want to be a boxer who had taken that one fight too many.

I never had any regrets. I've never been one for 'ifs' and 'buts', but I know that if it hadn't been for all the problems that I'd had with my broken hand, I could have gone a lot further than I had. But, there again, that's an 'if', and I may be very wrong. What I must say, if only to be fair to myself, is that in all my fights I never fought anyone with anywhere near as little experience as myself, and the majority of my fights were either top of the bill or chief supporting contests. Many times in the twelve months after I finished boxing, my ex- manager and others tried their best to entice me to make a come-back, but once I make a decision I stick to it.

Having said that, early in 1958, when I was still working for my dad, there was a professional boxing show in Haverfordwest. I had intended going to the show as a spectator, as my, ex-manager had a few fighters on the bill. On the afternoon of the show, he came to visit us at the nursery and told me (which I knew to be true) that one of his fighters had been injured in training and that he had been unable to replace him at the last minute. He knew that I always kept myself fit and asked me if I would take his fighter's place. Incidentally, I still had my professional boxer's licence. Because it was a local show, and professional boxing was a rare event in Pembrokeshire, not to let anyone down, I agreed. I boxed Danny Larty from Ghana and beat him on points over six rounds. At least, for what it was worth, I had finished with a victory. No, it did not make me change my mind. I had made my decision and I was sticking to it.

Many years have gone by since those days, and much water has passed under the bridge, but they are times that I have never regretted, and days that I can look back on with much pleasure and happy memories. Much has been said and written against boxing, but I believe that the majority of it can be put down to ignorance; I mean that in the nicest way. Yes, it's a tough sport and I don't think that anyone can deny that it can be dangerous, but then, so can many other things in life. If a boxer is properly trained and the very strict medical rules are adhered to, I believe that the risk is minimal.

I will argue with anyone that boxing has saved far more people than it has harmed. It has taken young boys off the streets in many parts of the world and taught them to make something of their lives. It helps to build their characters and teaches them self- control. In boxing, you don't see the childish tempers and pettiness that you see in professional football, for instance. I admit that I have little or no interest in boxing these days, but that does not mean that I do not look back on those days as part of life's education. You see, you must remember your past, to know where you are going in the future.

Bryn and Sybil in 1951

Bryn and Sybil on their Wedding Day

CHAPTER FOUR
JOINING THE POLICE FORCE

In 1951, Sybil and I had got engaged. I can never remember asking her to marry me and I am sure that I never did. It was something that we just took for granted and knew that we always would. Sybil's cousin, whose husband was in the Royal Navy, invited us down to Plymouth for a week's holiday, and we decided to get engaged when we were down there.

We had obviously told our parents, and had had their blessing.

On the way down to Plymouth by train, we had to change trains at Temple Meads Station, Bristol, and I well remember sitting on the platform at Bristol waiting for our connection, little knowing that one day we would be living in Bristol and that two of our grandchildren would be born there.

I bought Sybil's engagement ring in a shop in Plymouth for the princely sum of £42 and, believe me, that nearly left me broke. One day, Sybil and I and her cousin went by bus to Devonport to see the naval ships. When we were over there, I saw a pair of socks in a shop window and decided to buy them. In the shop, when I went to pay for the socks, I put my hand in my pocket for my wallet and found that it wasn't there. Before I could panic, I remembered that I had left it on the arm of a chair in Sybil's cousin's house. We managed to scrape together enough money between us to pay for the socks, but then had to walk more than half way home, because we did not have enough money for the bus fares from where the shop was.

Two years later, on 15th August 1953, Sybil and I got married in a little country church in Manorowen, which is about a mile from Goodwick on the St David's road. We were both regular members of the mother church, St Peter's in Goodwick, and our wedding was officiated by the vicar, Reverend Vernon Johns, who was a very good friend of ours.

Ours wasn't a big wedding, we could not afford it-only members of our immediate families.

We went to London for our honeymoon, by train. When we left on the train, after our small reception, we had less than £45 between us, after we had paid our return train fares. In London, we stayed for a week in a good-class guest house in Norfolk Square. We visited all the usual sights in London, went for two trips on the River Thames to Greenwich and to Kew Gardens.

We went to a show nearly every evening, bought a motor-cycle jacket each at Pride and Clarke's, and had a few bob (10-pence pieces) in our pocket when we arrived home. Imagine being able to do that today.

We started our married life in a rented flat over the Post Office in Main Street, Goodwick, right opposite the police station. Living in the police station then was Inspector Albert Cousins who, co-incidentally was my first boss when I joined the police force six years later and was posted to Pembroke Dock. Of course, the police station in Goodwick has been long gone and replaced by a new one in Fishguard, about a mile away. In 1955, we bought our first house in Park Street, Goodwick. It was a terraced house with three bedrooms but no bathroom when we bought it. It was right next to the only school I ever went to. We paid £800 for the house and had a council grant towards building a bathroom and a bigger kitchen. Our mortgage was £4.3.4d a month (about £4.17p). It was in a single row of 12 houses, which I believe had been built for £1200, that's about £100 each house. Today, they are being sold for £30,000 plus, each. When we sold the house in December 1959, when I joined the police force, we had £1600 for it, and we had to pay back to the council the £90 grant which we had had. By then, we had built a new bathroom and kitchen and, with the price which we had received for it, we thought we were millionaires.

I had actually finished working for my father in 1958 and, after much thought and discussion with Sybil, I decided to join the regular army. I visited the Army Recruiting Centre in Haverfordwest, where I was informed that, with my sporting background, I'd have no trouble getting into the Army Physical

Training Corps, after I'd finished my initial training, which was my main objective. I already held an Honours Diploma in Physical Training. I was also told at the Recruiting Centre that I would have no trouble in getting married quarters.

I went for my initial training to the South Wales Borderers Barracks at Brecon. In no time I was totally disillusioned. At the barracks, I was attending educational classes with fellow soldiers, many of whom couldn't write their own name. The lessons that we were receiving would have been more suited to children in an infants' school.

I complained, and they put me on a higher grade, which was almost as bad.. I know that I did not have a great educational background, but this was ridiculous, and I felt very degraded.

Things got worse when I was officially informed that it would be at least four years before I would be given married quarters.

I immediately asked for an interview with my commanding officer and told him that I had been grossly misinformed at the recruiting centre and that I wanted to be discharged from the army. He told me that I would have to pay to be discharged, and did his best to make me change my mind. When he could see that I was determined, he asked me to go home for the weekend and talk it over with my wife. I told him that I had not made my decision lightly and that I would not change my mind, but he insisted that I went home for the weekend. I did this, but came back in the same frame of mind on the Monday morning. I could have lived with the degrading education classes, but being separated from my wife and family for four years was not on. It cost me £20 to get my discharge. A small price for peace of mind.

I was never one to be out of work and soon got a job down in Milford Haven, where they were building the new Esso Oil Refinery. I joined a gang of labourers who used to travel down by van each day from Goodwick. Two of my good mates in the gang were Evan Thomas and George Walters. The van belonged to Evan, but I did most of the driving, so that they could have a couple of pints on the way home after a hard day. We were working 7am to 7pm and, with the travelling, it meant a 14 -

hour day. Our gang was engaged in digging a trench in solid rock down near the sea for the erection of a big dam. All the digging was by hand, using jack-hammers and shovels. It was really tough work, which suited me down to the ground.

I have never been one to think above my station in life but, the whole time that I was there, I kept thinking that I could do better for myself than this, and I was determined that I would.

By about the end of twelve weeks, although enjoying the physical side of the job, I was getting mentally fed up with a job that had no prospects. I did not want to pack in the job of my own accord. I would have seen that as a sign of weakness on my part. The decision was made for me at the end of that week, when the foreman came to us with what he thought was bad news, telling us that the job was finishing that weekend. To be honest, under my breath I said, 'Thank God.'

Again, not to be out of work, I started a job as a salesman/ collector with S & U Stores, a catalogue firm. My round covered the south of the county and consisted of calling on customers to collect their weekly instalments and to encourage them to buy more goods. I only took the job as a stop- gap, and I had many customers from whom I never took a penny the whole 12 weeks I was in the job. They would give me a sob story, saying their husbands were on the sick and they couldn't afford the payments this week and that they would pay next week. I would feel sorry for them and tell them not to worry. Not very businesslike I agree, but I didn't have the heart to do otherwise. The whole 12 weeks that I was with S & U Stores, I had no idea what the future had in store for me up until the day I put my notice in.

If I hadn't, they would have probably given me the push in any case.

People often ask me how I came to join the police force and, to be quite honest, I often wonder myself. It was something that happened completely out of the blue.

At the time, I was still working as a salesman/collector with S & U Stores. It was a job that I was not really interested in, but better than being on the dole. I had to go to Haverfordwest one day to meet my area manager at 4pm. I've always had a reputation for being early and arrived in Haverfordwest at about 2pm. I drove my car into the Riverside car park and then suddenly thought, 'What the hell am I going to do for the next two hours? 'With nothing much else to do in the county town, I thought that I would go up to the Police Headquarters, which was in the old castle in those days, and have a chat with some of the policemen. Many of them knew me from my days' boxing in the booth at the fairgrounds.

I parked my car in the Headquarters car park and went into the general office where I found Inspector Roberts and Sergeant Townsend. The sergeant looked up and said, Cor, Bryn Phillips! What can we do for you?' I told them that I'd come to give myself up as they had been trying to catch for so long. They both had a laugh, and then we started chatting, mostly about boxing. After I'd been there about twenty minutes, one of then said, 'By the way, what can we really do for you?' Without thinking, I said, 'I've come to join the police force.'

They both took me at my word and began telling me about the process of applying, getting references, etc. The more they went on, the more guilty I felt, as I realised they had taken me seriously. They went on about going away to police training school and gave me an application form and other leaflets. I suddenly looked up at the clock on the wall and saw that it was 3.45pm. I said. 'Hell, I've got to go.' They thrust the leaflets and application form into my hands and I dashed out of the door feeling extremely guilty.

When I returned to Goodwick at about 6pm, I thought I'd call to see my mum and dad before going home. Like all mums, she said, 'Sit down and have a cup of tea before going home.'

They were both sat at the table having their tea, and I sat down with them. When I was drinking my cup of tea, I remembered the forms etc. that they had given me at the Police Headquarters. I took them out from my pocket, saying to my dad that I'd called on the police and told them for fun that I was thinking of joining the police force. My dad looked at the forms and said, 'Hey, this isn't a bad idea.' I took the forms back from him and said, 'Don't you start', shouted , 'Cherrio' to my mum and dad and went home to Sybil and the baby.

I had my tea and then played with the baby for a while before she went to bed, and then Sybil and I sat down listening to the radiogram, as we couldn't afford a television at the time. It must have been about 10pm when I remembered the papers in my pocket and having called at the police headquarters. I got the papers from my jacket pocket, and Sybil and I started looking at them. It was really the first time that I had properly looked at them. After reading them through and talking to Sybil about the prospect, I began to think that it was not a bad idea after all. I asked Sybil what she thought of the idea and, as usual, she said that if it was what I wanted she would support me all the way. I did not take my thoughts too seriously, as I did think that my educational background was good enough.

A couple of days after I sent in my completed application form, together with three references from Mr Lake, my former school headmaster, the Reverend Vernon Johns, the vicar of St Peter's Church and Mrs Timothy, a local magistrate, a police constable called at the house in the evening and asked if I cou'd be at Goodwick Police Station the following morning to take a written examination. Next morning, at the police station, I sat the exam' in English, Maths, Geography and General Knowledge with Inspector (as he was then) Winston Jones.

Again, two days later, I was asked if I could be at the Police Headquarters, Haverfordwest, on the Saturday morning for an interview with Mr George Terry, the Chief Constable. I honestly never thought for one moment that I would be accepted and, at the best, thought that I might be told that I would hear something from them in a few months. At the interview with Mr Terry, he told me that he was accepting me as a constable and shook my hand. Half an hour later, in the offices of the Western Telegraph, I was sworn in by Mrs Lloyd, the proprietor of the newspaper, who was also a local magistrate. Back at the police headquarters, I telephoned the area manager of S & U Stores and told him that I was giving my notice as from then. I did not feel guilty, as they had always refused to give me a contract of employment. As impossible as it might seem today, the following Monday, 12 days after I had first walked into the police headquarters at Haverfordwest, on the pretence of wanting to join the police force, I was on my way to Bridgend to start a 13-week police training course.

Bryn's three daughters Marianne, Lydia and Jeannette in 1970

Bryn (3rd left) with his mum and dad and three brothers

CHAPTER FIVE
MY FIRST POSTING

When I joined the Police Force on 29th November 1959, before going away to the Police Training Centre in Bridgend for my 13-week Initial Training Course, we decided to put our house on the market, and put an advert in the local paper. We did not bother with Estate Agents in those days. We thought that if we could sell the house whilst I was away in the Training Centre, Sybil and Marianne, who was then 2 years and 3 months old, could move in with her parents and take a chance that we would have a police house when I finished my training. At that time Sybil was pregnant with our second child. Well, we had an offer for the house the first week that I was at the training centre, and we clinched the deal when I came home that weekend. A few weeks later we put our furniture into storage, and Sybil and Marianne moved in with her parents.

When I was at the training centre, I found myself to be the 'daddy' of the course of 27 recruits.

At the age of twenty eight-and-a-half I was a good bit older then most of the others on the course. Having left school over 14 years before, and having done little or no paper work all that time, I found it quite difficult at first studying law and different Acts of Parliament. When most of the others spent their evenings relaxing and enjoying themselves, I knuckled down to more studying, determined to make the most of the decision I had made. I am glad to say that the extra work that I put in paid off, and I came 4th in the final exams.

In those days, probably because it was a 13-week course, we could come home every weekend, except for one, when we had to do switchboard duty at the training centre. My weekend duty happened to be the week before our second baby was due. On the Sunday afternoon of that weekend, I was lying on my bed in my billet, which was in a wooden hut in those days. I was doing a bit of extra studying, having done my stint on the switchboard. I heard footsteps running across the yard outside. I could then see a hand tapping the window, which was high up, and heard a voice shouting, ' Bryn, you've got a baby daughter.' I shouted back, 'Yes, I know', meaning my daughter Marianne, and thinking that it was one of the boys pulling my leg, because they all knew that Sybil was expecting the baby. He came into the billet and convinced me that my mother-in-law was on the telephone, so I rushed over to the office to speak to her. No, he hadn't been pulling my leg, and she told me that Sybil had give birth to our second daughter that morning. I was relieved and delighted. I could have had compassionate leave to go home, but I reluctantly decided against it as it was out final exams the following week, and I was studying hard as I wanted to do well. As it was, our second daughter, who we named Lydia, was a week old when I first saw her.

The following week I was notified that I was being posted to Pembroke Dock and that I would have to go into lodgings, as there wasn't a police house available. I was quite disappointed, as for some reason I had bad ideas about Pembroke Dock, which goes to show how wrong one can be. After finishing my course at the training centre, I did a week's local procedure course at Police Headquarters, Haverfordwest, and on the Saturday, travelled to Pembroke Dock to begin my actual duty as a policeman.

My lodgings were with a Mrs Trotter in Front Street, Pembroke Dock. She was a lovely lady and immediately made me feel at home. The police station was in Charlton Place and a new station was almost completed in Water Street. In fact, we moved in there three weeks later. I finished my tour of duty that first day at 6pm and, on looking at the duty rota, saw that I was on Rest Day the following day, and on 6pm to 2am on the Monday. I immediately went back to my lodgings, had a quick cup of tea with Mrs Trotter, jumped in my car, and rushed down to Hobbs Point to catch the ferry to Neyland. Of course, that was long before the Cleddau Bridge was built. Before eight o'clock, I was home with Sybil and the children.

On the Monday, I started my first full tour of duty as a policeman, accompanied by a colleague, P. C. Les Froggatt, who, incidentally, is still a very good friend of ours today. In fact, Les and his wife Rene have a caravan on the Gower Peninsula, close to where we have ours. We often meet up, especially in the summer months. Again, on the Tuesday, I was accompanied on my tour of duty by another constable, but after that I was out on my own. Some might describe it as, 'being thrown in the deep end' but, at least, it meant that you had to get used to knowing your job pretty quick.

We did all our tours of duty on foot in those days, which is what I call proper Community Policing. The job was so different then. On the night shift one of our duties was to physically check all lock-up business premises to ensure that they were secure. There were always only two constables on the night tour of duty. One would be in the station on the switchboard, and the other out on foot patrol, changing over after a few hours. The sergeant was only on duty until 2am, so after that, the one constable was covering the town on his own.

Being constantly on foot patrol gave us the opportunity to get to know members of the public so much easier, because we were meeting them and speaking to them every day. Police today are so remote from the general public that it's no wonder why there is such a divide between the police and the public.

I had been stationed in Pembroke Dock for only two weeks, when I read in Force Orders that I had been allocated a police house in Cromwell Street. My tour of duty that day couldn't finish quick enough, so that I could drive home to Goodwick and tell Sybil the good news.

We moved in to our police house the following week and felt that we were a family again and could look forward to the future.

Our eldest daughter, Marianne, started school in Pembroke Dock, at Albion Square School. I really enjoyed my three and a half years there and we were very happy, despite my initial thoughts of the place. Sybil and I made a lot of good friends there, both in and out of the police.

Another reason, which gives us happy memories of Pembroke Dock, is the fact that our youngest daughter, Jeannette, was born there.

I have always considered that Pembroke Dock was an excellent place to start a career in the police force. It presented such a wide variety of police work. At that time it was a garrison town with a large army presence. There were Royal Naval ships in the dockyard, and they were starting to build oil refineries in the south of the county, which brought large numbers of labourers into the area.

As the Pembrokeshire Police was run in those days, every police officer had a good grounding in every aspect of police work. Whatever you encountered during your tour of duty, you dealt with. Obviously, you were given help with the more difficult cases, but it was a way of building one's confidence and competence. We even prosecuted our own cases in court, apart from the more complex ones.

I was, of course, stationed in Pembroke Dock when the first German Panzer Troops came to train at the tank ranges at Castlemartin Camp. At the time there was a big anti-German feeling in the country, and a huge anti-German demonstration was staged in Pembroke Dock, with thousands of demonstrators coming from all over the country. The German troops kept coming every year after that, and the anti-German feeling soon faded and they became an integral part of the community in the south of the county. In fact, many local girls married German soldiers. I feel that it was a great loss, both financially and otherwise, when they left for good in 1996.

In the early 1960's, Pembrokeshire Police was one of the very few police forces in the country that didn't have police dogs. The Chief Constable, Mr George Terry, had for some time been trying to convince the Police Committee to agree that police dogs would be a great asset to the force. It was in 1963 that they agreed with his views, and it was decided that the force would have two dogs.

When it was published in Force Orders, and applications were invited for the posts of dog handlers, I immediately applied. As I've said, I'd always had a good rapport with animals and I thought that this would be something that would give me job satisfaction. Some weeks later, I was informed that my

58

application had been successful and I was to be one of the two dog handlers. At that time, Glamorgan Police Dog Section had bred a litter of pups from one of police dogs at their kennels in Bridgend and our force had been given the offer of buying the last two pups in the litter.

My colleague, John Richards, who had been chosen as the other dog handler, and myself were sent to Bridgend to collect the two pups, which were then four months old. We found that one was a bitch pup and the other a dog. It was decided that I would have the bitch pup. The pups had already been named Ace and Asta. Although the official name of my pup was Pemcon Asta, I decided to call her Abi, and that's what she was always known as. I was, of course, still stationed and living in Pembroke Dock, and my colleague, John, was stationed and living in Haverfordwest.

It was arranged that both of us with our dogs would go to Bridgend every two weeks to meet up with the Glamorgan police dog handlers, to familiarise ourselves with police dog work before going away to a police dog training school. My three children were very young at the time, and you can imagine this young, boisterous dog growing up with them. I think it did the dog and the children a lot of good.

It was in the August that I was posted to Haverfordwest, to live in one of the two new police houses that had been built with permanent kennels for the police dogs.

We had been informed that we would be going to the Home Office Police Dog Training School in Stafford for our initial training as police dog handlers.

Although I'd had plenty of experience with dogs of my own before joining the police force, I knew that this was going to be something entirely different, and I was determined to make a success of being a dog handler. It was on a Sunday, 8th September 1963, that I left home with my dog, Abi, in the back of the car, and travelled to Stafford to begin my career as a dog handler. What of the future? I had that feeling that I was going to enjoy it.

There were 18 of us with our dogs on the course, from several different police forces, After the first two weeks of mostly obedience training, we were getting involved in the more advanced tracking and searching exercises. At this time it was a good idea to double-up with a colleague, so that we could lay each other's tracks and hide up for each other's dog, in the search for person training. In those days we used to do most of our training in the fields that were opposite the Dog Training School at Police Headquarters on the Cannock Road. Of course, those fields have been long gone and have become the vast Wildwood Housing Estate. Dog handlers training at Stafford today have to go much further afield to find training venues.

One lovely sunny day during the course I was doubled up with a colleague, John Towlson, from Nottingham, with his dog, Bruce. Incidentally, John and I are still very good friends today. We were training about three-quarters-of-a-mile from the dog school and were having a sit down, having just completed a training track each with our dogs. After a short rest, it was our intention to do some 'search for person' exercises in the nearby woods. As we sat on a grassy bank talking, both our dogs were playing nearby. As I was talking to John, I happened to look past him at his dog, which was playing with a solid rubber ball. As I was looking at the dog, I actually saw it swallow the ball.

The dog suddenly started clawing frantically at its mouth. I said to John, 'The dog's swallowed the ball', and we both went immediately to the dog. Although the dog was big and hairy, we could actually see the swelling of the ball stuck in its throat. By now the dog was frantic, and there were lots of blood and saliva coming from its mouth. It was also having difficulty, breathing. John got hold of the dog's jaws and prised its mouth open wide, while I put my hand down its throat to try and retrieve the ball. Whilst I could reach the ball easily, which by now was very slippery with saliva, as soon as I grasped the ball in my hand, my closed hand with the ball inside was too big for me to pull it out. As I tried to do so, it obviously hurt the dog and I had to leave the ball go. In doing so the dog bit me badly,

60

although John was still trying to hold its jaws apart. We tried this twice, and I got badly bitten each time, because the dog was very frightened, not knowing what was happening.

By now the dog was getting weaker all the time, and I honestly thought it was going to die.

With this in mind, and not wanting John, who by now was very upset, having to see his dog die, I suggested to him that he went back to the school to get some help. To my relief, he went.

The dog was now in a very weak state, and gasping for breath. Although I was bleeding badly from my hand, I couldn't stand there doing nothing. I grabbed hold of the dog and struck it a couple of times on the side of the head with my fist, and the dog slumped to the ground. Now that the dog was unconscious, it was easy to put my hand down its throat and pull the ball out, all its muscles being relaxed. For a moment I thought the dog was dead, because it was so still and quiet. Suddenly, it gave a few rasping breaths and shook, and, in a minute or so, was sitting up as if nothing had happened.

After about twenty minutes, I saw a Land Rover approaching and John arrived with one of the instructors and a couple of dog handlers. He couldn't believe his eyes when he saw his dog Bruce sitting alongside my dog. I must have looked a terrible sight. I was covered in blood, some my own, and some the dog's, where it had been clawing at its mouth. It was quite a warm day and I'd been sweating, and, wiping my brow with my hand, must have covered my face with blood as well. I was taken to the hospital to have my hand seen to, and when I got back to police headquarters, to my embarrassment, everybody made a fuss of what I'd done. I'm sure that John had exaggerated, when telling them what had happened. A few days later I had a written commendation from the Staffordshire Police Chief Constable, Mr Stanley Peck, and I subsequently was awarded the RSPCA Bronze Medal.

When my colleague, John Richards, and I came back from the Police Dog Training School at Stafford with our newly trained police dogs, they created quite a bit of interest in the Force and with the general public. Obviously much was expected of them, and they were put to use at every opportunity. As well as being a great asset in the prevention and detection of crime and hooliganism, they also had their public relations role to play.

Although we only had two dogs, we used to put on police dog displays at various events all over the force area, which were always well received by the public. In fact, they were in such demand that we couldn't fulfil all the requests we had.

My first success with my dog was when a wholesale fruit store on the outskirts of town was broken into. I was called to the scene with my dog. I cast the dog to see if she could pick up a track outside the broken window. She immediately picked up a scent, which she followed around the back of the premises and into a small woods where we found a broken-open orange box and some orange peel on the ground. She continued past the broken box and out of the woods towards the main road. She crossed over the main road and then up to the doorway of a cottage. A youth living at the cottage was later arrested by the CID for theft of fruit from the store.

I remember well August Bank Holiday, 1965. Neither John nor myself was on duty because there was no need for dog handlers on a Bank Holiday in those times, but I was the duty dog handler on call. About mid-afternoon, my wife and I were playing with the children in the park at the rear of our house, when we heard the telephone ringing. Sybil ran into the house to answer the telephone and then I heard her shout to me that the Control Room Sergeant wanted me. On going to the phone, he told me to go immediately to Tenby, because there were dozens of 'Mods' and 'Rockers' fighting on the beach. Believe me, he took a minute or so to convince me that he was telling the truth, because we had never had that kind of trouble before. On realizing that he was genuine, I put the dog into the dog van and in less than half an hour I was in Tenby.

I arrived at the end of the Esplanade and, on looking down towards the South Beach, I could see that the forecourt in front of the cafe was full of people fighting. All the holiday makers and their children had retreated onto the sands, and were

62

terrified. I took the dog out from the van, put her on the leash and ran down the footpath towards the cafe.

When I was near the bottom of the footpath, with the dog pulling hard on the leash, I must have inadvertently pressed the quick- release clip on the leash, because the dog shot forward towards the fighting crowd. I am not exaggerating, when I say that, within a matter of seconds, there wasn't a single person in the forecourt of the cafe, and there was spontaneous applause from the holiday makers on the beach.

I know that is not the correct way in which police dogs should be used, and I am sure that many did not believe me when I said that I had not purposely released the dog, but the fact remains that all the trouble was stopped in seconds. We did not receive any complaints from anyone having been bitten by the dog, although I know that many had been.

I had a call late one evening from the Control Room of a young boy missing from the caravan in which he lived with his parents on a farm. I immediately turned out and went to the farm, which was about half an hour journey away. On arrival at the farm, I met P. C. Don Evans, a patrol car driver, who had first attended the call, and the young boy's parents.

The parents were obviously very anxious about their boy, who was nine years old. They explained that they had sent the young boy to bed early because he had been naughty. Before going to bed themselves at about half past ten, they had looked in the boy's bedroom to see if he was OK and found that his bed was empty and the bedroom window open. The father, who was the farm manager, and the owner of the farm had searched all the farm buildings and the surrounding area before calling the police to report him missing. The father explained to me that he did not think that the boy had gone far, as he was pretty much afraid of the dark.

Although it was now nearly midnight, there was a full moon, so visibility was very good. I explained to the boys parents that I was going to do a free search with the dog, which meant that I was going to set the dog loose to search the area, to try and pick up the boy's body scent. Leading from the farmyard, not

63

far from where the caravan was parked, was a gateway into a very large field full of stooks of corn. That was the way in which corn was harvested in those days.

I asked the boys parents, the patrol car driver and the farmer to stay by the gate, and I gave the dog the command to search. She immediately shot off down the field through the stooks of corn and was soon lost from sight. I stood there quietly with the group, and I'm sure that they did not think very highly of my method of searching for the missing boy. We had been standing there for three or four minutes, with everyone looking rather anxious, when in the distance we heard the dog barking. It was obviously quite some distance away. I dashed off in the direction of the barking, after telling the group they could follow me if they wished. Every now and again I would stop and listen. There was silence. I would shout the command, 'Where is he', and the dog would bark again for a few seconds. When near the bottom of the field, I again stopped and shouted a command to the dog. She barked again not far away, and I shone my powerful torch towards the sound, and could see the back end of the dog sticking out from one of the stooks of corn, as if she was pulling something. On reaching the stook, we saw that the dog had hold of the foot part of a Wellington boot and was attempting to pull the young boy out from the middle of the stook where he had been sleeping. The group immediately started clapping. The boy's parents, obviously relieved, also looked amazed, which at the time surprised me, as, after all, the dog had only done what it had been trained to do. I must say that this was another example of a trained dog doing, in a matter of minutes, what it would have taken a large number of man-hours to do, and maybe without the same result.

I received a call late one very stormy night to look for a missing man. He lived on his own in a very lonely cottage way off the beaten track. He had been due to appear in court that day on a charge of drink driving but had not turned up. When the local policeman had gone to the cottage that evening, he had found the man's car outside the cottage with a note inside, indicating that he intended doing himself some harm.

When I arrived at the scene it was getting on for midnight and the weather couldn't have been worse. It was blinding down with rain and blowing a gale. The local policeman, George Mortimer was present and he put me in the picture, stating that there was some concern as to the man's well-being. He gave me a rough idea of the surrounding area, as best he could, and, of course, it was pitch dark, as we were well away from any roads with street lights.

Obviously, the time lapse and weather conditions were not conducive with putting the dog to try and pick up a track from the man's car, so I decided to do a free search with the dog. I asked George if he could stay at the scene and gave my dog the command. 'Find him', and she shot off into the darkness. I had a very powerful torch with me, which was much needed, and I stumbled off into the blinding rain in the direction in which the dog had gone, occasionally shouting the command, 'Find him'.

After about ten minutes stumbling forward in the pitch dark, I heard my dog barking some considerable distance away. Not knowing the area, I kept going forward in the direction of the now continuous barking. Shining my torch ahead of me, I could see a woods and what appeared to be a light, swinging back and forth amongst the trees. At this point I had come to some very marshy ground and had to make a detour to get around to where the dog was barking. As I got near the wood, I again shone my torch and it again appeared as if there was a light swinging amongst the trees.

As I approached to where the dog was barking, I could see her jumping up at something, and it was then that I saw the body of a man, hanging from the branch of a tree. The body was wearing a new pair of Wellingtons and the dog had been jumping up with her front feet against the Wellingtons, making the body swing. What I had thought to be a light had been the reflection of my torch on the wet boots. I immediately cut the man's body down, but could see that he had been dead for some considerable time. Had it not been for the dog, we would probably not have found the poor soul until daylight.

Bryn when he was a dog handler in Dyfed Powys Police

Chapter Six
Climbing the Ladder

When at the Police Dog Training School, we had been told of the police dog trials, which are held each year in order to assess and maintain the required standard of efficiency of police dogs. The trials are first held at Force level, then at Regional level, and culminate at the National Police Dog Trials, at which the best 20 odd dogs in the country compete.

I was always determined that my dog would maintain a high standard of proficiency and took every opportunity I could to give the dog the required training. In those days we were allowed one day per fortnight as a training day. I was also fortunate that the police house at which I lived was near to fields and woodland, which meant that I did not have to travel any distance in order to train the dog. I have often come home at the end of a day's training and, if my dinner was not ready, I would take the dog out into the fields for some more training, until my wife called that my meal was ready.

By 1968, when the Pembrokeshire Police amalgamated with the Carmarthen and Cardigan Constabulary and the Mid- Wales Police to become the Dyfed Powys Police, I had been a dog handler for five years, and, apart from having a good number of arrests with my police dog, Abi, we had also won the Welsh Region Police Dog Trials in 1966 and 1967, qualifying for the National Police Dog Trials both years at Malvern and Glasgow respectively. There were no police dog trials in 1968 because of an outbreak of Foot and Mouth Disease.

In the meantime, I had also passed my police promotion examination to the rank of Sergeant, my total marks being one of the highest 200 in the country.

With the event of the amalgamation and, with the increase in the size of our Dog Section, it was natural of me to assume that we were now a big enough section to warrant having a Sergeant in charge, and, with my experience and record, the likelihood of me being at least considered for the post.

I went to work one day and read in Force Orders that one of the dog handlers in Carmarthen had been promoted Sergeant in Charge of the Dog Section. I must admit that I felt rather disappointed and let down, as he had been a dog handler for a very short time and had very little experience with police dogs. I obviously did not hold this against him and always gave him my full support as my sergeant.

At the beginning of 1969, whilst still very much enjoying my duties as a dog handler, I felt that there was little or no future for me in the force, so I decided to apply to become a dog handler in the Metropolitan Police. They obviously knew of me by reason of my competing in Regional and National Police Dog Trials, as, in a very short time, I had a reply informing me that my application had been successful and asking me to attend at London for a medical examination. At this time, things were in full swing for the 1969 Regional Police Dog Trials, which for our Region, was for that year being organised by the Gwent Police. To be completely honest, I really did not want to compete that year, much as I enjoyed the event, and I told then so at Headquarters. I was overruled and was ordered to take part.

In March, I went away to the trials in Gwent with Sergeant Ken Davies, our new Dog Section Sergeant, who was attending as an observer. I don't have to tell anyone that it would have been so easy for me to have felt bitter and to have done badly at the trials, without any suspicion falling on me. Except for one thing - my pride. I was a Pembrokeshire dog handler and we were not going to let Pembrokeshire down. Once again, for the third year running, Abi and I became Welsh Region Police Dog Champions.

As far as I was concerned, this was my Swan Song. I had a letter in my pocket telling me that I had been accepted as a dog handler in the Metropolitan Police. I was never one to sit back and reflect if things were not going right, but to get up and do something about it. On the last day of the Dog Trials, at the Presentation Dinner, I was told by Sergeant Davies that he had received a telephone message from Headquarters in Carmarthen, saying that I was to call at Headquarters on my way home the following day, as the Chief Constable wanted to see me.

Abi, 3 times Welsh champion

Bryn with his first Police dog Abi

Bryn with Abi at the Police dog trials

My Sergeant and I arrived at Headquarters late morning the following day. My colleague, John Richards, was there meeting me with our dog van, as I had been using one of the Headquarters dog vans to go to the Trials. As soon as John saw me, he was full of excitement and said, 'What have you been up to?' I looked at him in surprise, and said, 'Apart from the usual, John, nothing.' John said that he did not know what was going on but there had been a lot of speculation, and Chief Superintendent Richards of the Pembrokeshire Division had been summoned to Headquarters that morning.

Shortly afterwards, I was instructed to go to the Chief Constables office. I was, of course, dressed in civilian clothes, as I had been outside our Force Area. When I walked into the Chief's office I had with me my winner's Trophy and my Certificate of Competence. The Chief Constable was sat behind his rather large desk with Mr Thomas, the Deputy Chief Constable to his left, and then Chief Superintendent Richards, who was my Divisional Commander. I stood in front of the Chief Constable and said in my usual way, 'Good morning'. Not 'Sir', because as far as I was concerned, I was wishing them all good morning.

The Chief Constable looked at me and congratulated me on winning the Police Dog Trials, and said that I had brought honour on the Force. He did not sound very sincere to me. He then invited Mr Thomas to congratulate me and then Chief Superintendent Richards, which they did. I could see a smile in Chief Superintendent Richards' eyes. I knew that he was on my side.

After the congratulations, which on the whole did not sound very enthusiastic to me, the Chief Constable boomed at me, 'Now then, boy. Tell me why you have applied to join the Metropolitan Police. He, of course, knew of my application, because I had submitted a report informing him of my intention. I looked directly back at the Chief and said, 'Excuse me, Sir', and went over to a chair that was on my left, and put my trophy and certificate down on the chair. I don't know why I did that, probably to have my hands free. I returned to where I had originally been standing and said, 'Well, Sir, now that you have asked, I will tell you why.'

I started by explaining that Sergeant Davies had been with me all the week at the Regional Dog Trials and that I had spent much time passing on to him all my knowledge and experience with regard to the 'ins' and 'outs' of Police Dog Trials, and that there was certainly no bad feeling or bitterness as far as I was concerned. I went on to explain what I had put into the Dog Section over the years, and that, although my enthusiasm was still there, I could see no future for myself in the current circumstances. I said that there were two things that were very important to me in my life, my wife and family and my future.

He glared at me, and literally shouted across the desk, 'Now you listen to me, boy. 1 am promoting you to Sergeant from the 1st April (I thought, Christ, that's an appropriate date).

I am posting you to Pembroke in charge of the Country Stations, and you can live in the new house behind Pembroke Police Station, and you can keep your police dog and work her when you wish.'

I stood silent, without a flicker of emotion, and again he boomed, 'Well?' I replied, 'Well what, Sir?' 'What's your answer?' he said. 'I don't know, Sir', I replied, 'I haven't talked it over with my wife yet.' He nearly went through the ceiling, and Mr Thomas, the Deputy said, 'What's it to do with your wife?' I replied, 'Everything. I don't make decisions that's going to effect my family without talking it over with my wife.'

Now then, let's be practical. I'm a great believer in 'A bird in the hand ...!', and I knew before the Chief had finished talking, what my decision was, and I also knew for certain that my wife, being the wife she is, would support any decision I made. I knew that I was probably being petty, but I thought, 'Hell, why should I give them my answer now?' The Chief simmered down and asked me if I could go home and talk it over with my wife and come back in the afternoon with my answer. Although I knew that I was making it inconvenient for myself, I wasn't going to back down now and replied, 'Yes. Thank you, Sir.' Arriving home and telling my wife what the situation was, I knew word perfect what her answer would be.

72

It's history now that I changed into my police uniform, and drove all the way back to Carmarthen to give the Chief Constable the answer that I should have given him that morning. I walked out from Police Headquarters that afternoon, being the first Pembrokeshire Police Officer since amalgamation, to be promoted without being moved out of the county.

Having won the Welsh Region Police Dog Trials for 1969 meant that, once again, I had qualified for the National Police Dog Trials to be held that year in Ashford, Kent. The National Trials were in April, after I had been promoted Sergeant. Because of my promotion, I was, of course, no longer a member of the Dog Section, and when, later in the month, I competed in the National Police Dog Trials, it meant that I was the only person ever to compete in any Police Dog Trials, and not being a member of a Dog Section. No! Nothing to get excited about but at least unique.

When I moved to Pembroke in charge of the Country Stations, I also often worked in the towns of Pembroke and Pembroke Dock, which was, of course, my old training ground. I knew Pembroke Dock and it's people well, which made it much easier to carry out my duties.

They talk these days of Community Policing as if it is something rather new. I, of course, can only speak of Pembrokeshire, but when I joined the Police Force in 1959, and long before that, all policing in Pembrokeshire was community policing.

We walked the streets day and night and got to know everyone, and everyone got to know us.

I know that much has changed over the years: crime has increased, criminals have become more technical and mobile, and the police have to move with the times. But, I believe also, that, to a degree, they have moved too much in the wrong direction.

Of course there is a need for fast cars, helicopters and armed response vehicles in today's Police Force, but I strongly believe that there is still a genuine need for the policeman on the beat. Among other things, it will give back to the general public the confidence in the police that today is sadly lacking. I have been told that there have been ram-raids at night in Bristol that have not been discovered until the shop owners arrived to open up the following morning.

At night time, the noise made by these raids could be heard by a policeman on foot patrol quite some distance away. How can one expect them to be heard, when all the police on duty are driving around in cars? Even in these violent days, if the constable out on his own didn't want to confront the criminals without help , he has his personal radio to summon assistance.

I know that this is not the only reason by far that there is such an increase in crime, but I will take a lot of convincing that it is not one of the reasons.

When I was a sergeant in charge of the Country Stations in the south of the Pembrokeshire Police area, we had a call one day to where they were carrying out building work at the rear of a garage business in Sageston. The workmen, when using a mechanical digger on the site, had unearthed what they believed to be a bomb. A constable and myself attended the scene, and, on looking down into the trench, I could see a very rusty cylindrical object about three feet in length and about the circumference of a football. I could see that the object had fins on one end. I must admit that to me, because of its rusty and muddy condition, the object looked quite harmless. Having said that, going by the book, I telephoned the police station at Pembroke Dock, informing them of the find and requesting them to inform the Bomb Disposal Unit at Hereford; first asking the workmen to stop working on the site, and for them not to disturb the object in any way.

A few hours later, an officer and sergeant from the Bomb Disposal Unit arrived on the site.

One of them carefully climbed down into the trench to examine the object, and shortly afterwards informed us that it was an unexploded German aerial bomb, obviously dropped during the bombing raids on the oil tanks at Pembroke Dock during the war. The officer asked me to arrange for all the dwellings within a radius of about 400 yards to be evacuated immediately. As I was carrying this out, I don't mind admitting that I thought that they were being a little over-cautious, but who was I.to argue with the experts?

When this was done, we all kept well out of the way, whilst the Bomb Disposal chaps went down into the trench with a few tools, one of which I noticed was a hand drill. After about half an hour, the officer came to me and informed me that the bomb had been made safe and that people could return to their homes.

He then asked me if there was anywhere suitable where the bomb could be taken to be detonated. Immediately, Castlemartin Tank Ranges sprang to mind, as it was on my patch. I telephoned the Adjutant at the camp and made the necessary arrangements. The bomb was loaded onto the Bomb Disposal units truck, and my constable and I escorted it to Castlemartin Camp.

At Castlemartin, the bomb was taken well out into the ranges, near the sea cliffs and well away from the camp itself. The Bomb Disposal men did what was necessary for a safe detonation, and we then all retreated to behind a rock bluff, about 400 yards from where the bomb had been placed. All the time, I kept thinking, was there really need for such caution? Then 'Bang', there was a terrific explosion, and huge boulders could be seen being hurled out into the sea.

The explosion had left a crater large enough to hold two double decker buses. Boy! did my admiration for those two guys change. I wasted no time in telling them so. To think that a short time before they had been crouched over that 'thing', using a hand drill to make it safe. I felt no shame in grabbing them both by the hand and letting them know what I thought of their courage.

Their first concern was to telephone home to say that the job was safely over. Aren't we fortunate to have guys like that?

I very much enjoyed being a sergeant in charge of the country stations in the south of the County, probably more so because I still had my police dog and could use her when needed. It was during this time that I had one of my best successes with my dog.

It was about 11-30pm on Christmas Eve 1970. I was off duty and home in the house behind the police station in Pembroke. My wife and eldest daughter, Marianne, were in church, our two other children were in bed and probably dreaming about Father Christmas. The telephone rang and it was one of my constables, Dudley Jones. He said that he was at a house in Manorbier with a sergeant from Tenby. He went on to say that the householders, a short time before, had been disturbed and found a man in the kitchen of their home. When challenged, the man had run out through the back door.

Dudley asked if I could attend with my police dog. I said to Dudley that my wife was in church; I would come as soon as she got home. Just at that moment, I heard footsteps coming down the yard from the police station, realised that it was my wife and said to Dudley that I was on my way. He told me to take care as it was foggy. About 20 minutes later I arrived at the house in Manorbier.

I went into the house to speak to the man and woman, living there, and to Dudley and the sergeant. I asked the householders to give me brief details of what had happened, and had to smile when they described how, when they were in bed, they heard a noise downstairs. The man of the house, who was over 6ft. tall, had told his wife to go down and see what the noise was. The woman, who was quite tiny, on entering the kitchen had discovered a man standing there. She said that on seeing her, the man had run out through the back door. She added that she did not know in which direction the man had gone on leaving the house.

I ascertained that no-one had been outside the back door since the intruder had left, got my dog from the car at the front of the house, and went back into the kitchen. I put the tracking harness and line on the dog and left the house the same way that the intruder had gone, giving the dog the command to 'seek.' She immediately tracked around to the front of the house, within the grounds, did a quick about turn, back past the back door and out onto the roadway.

She turned right on the roadway for a few yards, and then through a gap in the hedge into a field at the rear of the house.

76

Although now it was about 0030 hours on Christmas morning, and cloudy, there was a full moon and one could see pretty well. The dog tracked down the sloping field and into what appeared to be a large overgrown garden with a high stone wall on three sides. She tracked right around the wall and back out into the field, up the slope and over a stile into the adjoining field. As the dog tracked across this field, I could see on the far side the outline of two large detached houses, which the dog was tracking towards. When we were half way across the field, the dog suddenly stopped and stood absolutely rigid, just like a pointer dog.

I kneeled down beside the dog, looking in the direction of the two houses some 50-60 yards ahead. I realised that the dog had heard something and, on listening, I could hear a crunching sound.

The two houses were painted in a very light colour and, as I was listening, I suddenly saw someone run across the front of one of the houses. I immediately took the tracking harness off the dog and said, 'Get him'. She was off like a bullet, with me after her. As I ran forward, I saw the person double back across the front of the house, as if he had seen or heard us. At the same time, the dog took him in full flight, on his right arm. With him running, and the momentum of the dog hitting him, he fell flat on his face on the front lawn of the house.

As I approached, he kept struggling and shouting and, because of this, the dog held on to his arm. I got the man to his feet with the dog still hanging on, because he would not submit.

I would mention here that I was dressed in civilian clothing, and you can imagine two men and a dog struggling on the lawn in front of this big house, and with the intruder shouting and swearing. Suddenly, the downstairs bay window to the right of the front door of the house opened and an elderly lady started shouting, 'What are you doing on my lawn?' The more that she and the intruder kept shouting, the more excited the dog got, and would not let go of the man's arm.

In the quiet of the night, Dudley and the sergeant had heard all this commotion from the other house about quarter of a mile away, and I was very relieved when I saw the police van coming up the driveway of the big house towards me. By now the man had stopped struggling and the dog had let go of his arm. I asked the sergeant to go and explain to the elderly lady exactly what had happened. I told the man that he was being arrested on suspicion of burglary, cautioned him, and handed him over to the constable.

What had really happened was that, after leaving the first house, to which I had had the call, the man had come across the fields exactly the way that the dog had tracked, and had broken into the large house through the downstairs window to the left of the front door. On getting into the room, he had discovered that the door leading to the rest of the house was locked from the other side. What the dog and I had heard, was the crunching of the broken glass on the flower-bed beneath the broken window as the intruder was climbing back out, with the intention of breaking in by the other window. It was when he was in the process of doing this that he heard us coming, and the rest is now history.

Later that morning, Christmas Day, I had to go to the police station in Pembroke Dock to complete the paper work as arresting officer during the night's incident. The prisoner had been interviewed by the CID and had confessed to several more burglaries in the Manorbier area during the previous few weeks. He said that he had hidden most of the property that he had stolen, in rabbit holes and bushes, etc., but could not remember exactly where, as it was dark at the time. Being that he was a soldier from Manorbier Army Camp, I guessed that the property would be somewhere between the village and the Camp. I decided to make a search for the property with my police dog, and immediately left for Manorbier.

Knowing the area fairly well, I concentrated on an area of thick undergrowth not far from the Camp. In no time, the dog was showing indications, and I was utterly amazed at the amount of property that we recovered. There were small items of furniture, clothing, jewellery and various other household items. In all, almost a van load of property. The arrested person was subsequently found guilty of the burglaries and was given a prison sentence. If it were not for the police dog, it might have been quite some time, if ever, that these crimes would have been detected.

I was a Sergeant in Pembroke and Pembroke Dock when they started building the Cleddau Bridge. It was what I believe they call a box section type, where each section is built on site, and then transported, on a bogie on rails, out to the end of the part already built, and then lowered down into position and bolted and welded on the part already in place.

I was on duty one lovely sunny morning, patrolling Pembroke Dock with a young constable, Phil Lloyd, whose mother-in-law, incidentally, lived in Pembroke Ferry, where the bridge was being built. Because we did not have the personal radios, which they have today, I decided to call in at the police station to see if there was anything needed to be done. As we went into the front foyer of the station, where the inquiry hatch was, I could see through the hatch that there was no-one in the office and the telephone was ringing. I asked Phil to go in and answer the telephone. As Phil was speaking on the telephone, I could see him through the hatch and saw a look of shock on his face.

He suddenly looked across at me and shouted, 'The bridge has collapsed'. At first, I could hardly believe him, because we would pull each other's leg now and again. He then said that it was his mother-in-law on the telephone and, by the look on his face and his general demeanour, realised that he was telling the truth. Classing this as an emergency, I got the police van from the station yard and we immediately went to Pembroke Ferry.

When we arrived on the scene, there were people running about everywhere, and there was a huge cloud of dust, as the weather had been so hot and the ground bone dry. I could see the sections of the bridge that had already been built sloping down at a grotesque angle, with the end embedded in the ground. I immediately realised that this was a major incident, and telephoned all the emergency services. I remember crawling under the sloping bridge to see if there was anyone trapped underneath, and thankfully there was not.

79

Suddenly, I noticed that everything had gone very quiet. But, in a short space of time, all the emergency services were on the scene and got on with their duties. Sadly, there were a few workmen killed in the accident, and when the investigation into the cause of the collapse was carried out by structural engineers, they found that it was due to a large number of contributory factors.

On completion of the bridge, it meant, of course, that there was no further need for the ferry that had been running between Hobbs Point and Neyland for very many years. A loss , I feel, of a little more nostalgia.

Talking of Hobbs Point reminds me of one of the more tragic sides of police work. Late one evening, when I was a constable in Pembroke Dock, I was on my night shift, 10pm to 6am, and patrolling the town on foot, as we did in those days, when I met Sandy Buttle, the local youth leader. Sandy had a worried look on his face, and he was hurrying down towards the sea front. It must have been about 11pm.

He stopped to talk to me, and said that he was a little concerned because, earlier in the evening, one of the lads from the youth club had asked him if he could borrow one of the canoes to go across to Neyland to pick up one of his mates, who had missed the last ferry. Sandy said that had been hours ago, and that the lad had not come back. Seeing that Sandy was quite concerned, I decided to go down to Hobbs Point with him, at the same time trying to assure him that everything would be all right. At Hobbs Point, which at that time of night, was completely deserted, there was no sign of the lads nor the canoe. Because it was so quiet at that time of night, I was able to shout across the water, hoping that if they were at the water's edge on the Neyland side, they would be able to hear me, and put our minds at rest. Needless to say, there was no reply, and because of the time factor, I was beginning to get a little concerned myself.

By now, I had let my colleagues at the police station know of the situation, and a check was made at the youth club in case the canoe had been returned without them letting Sandy know and the lads had returned home. A check at both places proved negative. We went back down to Hobbs Point, and I called out a local boatman who lived nearby, who straight away volunteered to take us across to Neyland, in the hope of finding the canoe on the slipway close to where the ferry was moored, and the two lads somewhere in the vicinity, but this was not to be. I even went up into the town of Neyland in the hope of finding them, but there was no sign of anyone.

By now, others had joined us, and, in two boats, we started to search all the waterway between Neyland, Pembroke Ferry and Hobbs Point. There was a stiff breeze blowing off the Neyland side, which made the water very choppy between Pembroke Ferry and Hobbs Point. In the early hours of the morning, using powerful lamps, we found the canoe washed up on the rocks between Pembroke Ferry and Hobbs Point and, obviously now, we all feared the worst.

At about 6.30am, we broke off the search for a short rest and I went home to change into civilian clothes. It was beginning to get light about 7am, when we resumed the search. We had not been searching for long and I was standing at the bow of one of the boats, when I saw the body of one of the lads, floating submerged, about three feet under the surface of the water and about 200 yards off Hobbs Point. We recovered the body and about half an hour later, we found the body of the second lad lying on the sand, where the tide had gone out. Both bodies were fully clothed. Two young lives tragically lost, when one of them was doing a good turn.

It's a funny old world.

Police dog trials, although frowned upon by some, are an essential part of police dog work. All tests at the trials are set to be practical as near as possible and to simulate incidents which the handler and dog may encounter whilst on operational duty. The trials tests consist of Obedience, Agility, Searching for persons and for property, Tracking and Criminal work - that is, where the dog is trained to chase after and apprehend a fleeing criminal. There is also a police problem test to assess the dog handler's ability to deal with any incident.

81

The object of the trials is to maintain the standard of police dog work, and help in the further development of training methods.

Firstly, each force holds its own dog trials, in order to assess which handlers and dogs are going forward to represent the force in the Regional Police Dog Trials.

The Regional Trials are held annually and are organised by each force in the Region in turn.

The handlers and dogs winning the top places in each of the Regional Trials go forward to represent that Region in the National Police Dog Trials, which are held at one of five or six different venues in turn, annually. The number of handlers and dogs representing each Region is pro-rata to the number of dogs in the Region.

In April 1971, it was the turn of Dyfed Powys Police to organise the trials for the Region, which included all police forces in Wales and the South West of England. Although I was not then a member of the Dog Section, because of my previous experience with police dogs and Police Dog Trials, I was asked to assist in the organising and running of the trials. Although I was quite happy in my present role of Sergeant in Pembroke, getting back amongst the handlers and dogs for the week of the trials certainly aroused my desire to work again on a Police Dog Section.

Actually, when the trials had finished, I did not think too much more about it until, a few weeks later, an advert appeared in the 'Police Review' for a post of a Sergeant on the Dog Section of the Bristol City Police. It obviously aroused my interest, and I asked Sybil what she thought about it. It was a silly question really, because I always had her full support with whatever I did, and she said that if it was what I wanted, she would be happy. At that time, I was seconded to Tenby for the summer season, but of course I was still living in Pembroke.

Well, I applied for the post, and on the 1st July I had a letter from the Bristol Police, telling me that I had been short-listed and asking me to attend for an interview on 8th July 1971. On the day of the interview, I believe that I was the last candidate to be seen and, before leaving the Bristol City Police Headquarters, I was told that I had been successful and was offered the post, which I accepted.

During the next few weeks, before I left the Dyfed Powys Police, I informed the police in Bristol that I still had my police dog, Abi, who was in semi-retirement, and asked them, if I was to bring her with me, could I work her operationally in Bristol? They told me that they would be delighted for me to bring her, which resulted in giving her a new lease of life. I worked her operationally in Bristol for the next 18 months.

I also had a yellow Labrador of my own, which I had been given by an ex army officer who was a member of a civilian dog- training class, which I ran in Pembroke Dock. He had a yellow Labrador bitch, from which he bred a litter of pups. He insisted that I had the pick of the litter.

The pup I chose, I named Nimbus; it grew into a beautiful dog. I brought Nimbus to Bristol with me, hoping that the police would use it as a Drugs search dog, but they dithered so much in making up their minds, that I gave Nimbus to a friend of mine. Sadly, Nimbus was killed in a road accident shortly afterwards.

I will always remember the day that we actually moved to Bristol. The removal lorry had left, and, as I drove my car down the main street in Pembroke away from the police station, with Sybil beside me and the three girls in the back, I had a lump in my throat and I couldn't speak. I was thinking, 'My God, have I done the right thing?' Abi and Nimbus had gone ahead of us. They'd been collected by the Bristol Police a few days before.

Sybil and I knew that what lay ahead of us would be a challenge. Going from a county like Pembrokeshire, where we had always lived, to a large city like Bristol, it was obvious that we were going to find it a big difference from what we were used to. Still, we were going together, and that's what gave me the confidence. Of course, our three girls were still too young to be concerned. It was a big adventure to them. Although we

83

had left many good friends in Pembrokeshire, we soon made new ones in Bristol, and I can honestly say that we never regretted that initial move, but at the same time, we have always considered Pembrokeshire to be our home, and always will.

We all soon settled into our new life in Bristol, living for a few months in a police house and then buying our own. Our three girls soon settled into their respective schools and soon made new friends. Sybil, because the three girls were now in school, started working part-time in Marks and Spencer, a job which she enjoyed for the next 20 years. It gave her a chance to make new friends, and the hours she worked meant that she was always at home when the girls came home from school.

It was the 1st September 1971, when I commenced my duties on the Dog Section of the Bristol City Police and was stationed at Redland Police Station, which at the time was the base for the Mounted and Dog Sections. I was only there for a short time, because on the 10th September 1971, we moved down to the new purpose-built Mounted and Dogs Sections Headquarters at Bower Ashton, down below the Suspension Bridge near the Cumberland Basin. It was officially opened by the Duke of Beaufort on 19th September 1971.

Although I found police work in Bristol very different to that in Pembrokeshire, in a very short time I felt as if I had been there all my life. I think that you'll agree that life is what you make it. We were four Sergeants on the Dog Section, each with our own group of dog handlers. Our tours of duty were - days: 10am to 5pm, evenings, 5pm to midnight, and nights, midnight to 7am. We worked a seven hour tour of duty, as we were allowed one compensatory hour for caring for our dogs whilst off duty.

For my first two tours of duty in Bristol, which were evenings, I was doubled up with a constable dog handler. After that, I was on my own. Each dog handler covered a particular Division, but the Sergeants covered the whole of the city, supervising the whole group. Because of this, I had to get to know quickly how to find my way around Bristol, and I soon did.

As a Dog Section Sergeant, I had very little to do with the

Mounted Branch, other than being based at the same place. In spite of this, because of my love of horses, I probably took more interest in the work of the Branch, not realising for a moment how this would hold me in very good stead in the future.

In May 1972, my police dog, Abi, died. It caused much distress in the family. The three girls were broken hearted, and I took it quite badly myself. Working together every day for so long, one can get so attached. On 26th June, I started training a new dog called Skol. All the dogs in the Bristol Police were trained by themselves. They did not send the handlers away to a Police Dog Training School for training, not in those days anyhow. Although I was just as committed, I did not think that this new dog would ever take the place of Abi, or live up to her reputation.

That year, I joined the Soap Box Club, whose chairman was Charlie Chester. It was a voluntary organisation to help people who were in need. Obviously, the help given to the people cost them nothing, and in the majority of instances it was much appreciated by them, who, in many cases, couldn't afford the cost of having anything done, or were disabled in some way. It was reward enough seeing the look of gratitude on their faces when you did the little jobs for them.

Of course, you always get the odd one. I was wallpapering a room for a woman one day, I'd even got the wallpaper for her for nothing. I was up on the step ladder, struggling with an awkward piece of paper and she was standing nearby, telling me how well off her two sons were and what vast sums of money that were earning. She said that they gave her plenty, but she was putting it away for a rainy day. I thought, 'Hell, it should be raining today'. You always get a few that slip through the net.

In May 1973, we went on our first foreign holiday, to Lido di Jeslo in Italy. We flew from Luton Airport to Venice. We were members of the International Police Association and through them, the police in Lido di Jeslo knew that we were coming.

The first day that we were there, we were sat in the hotel lounge after dinner with all the other guests, when we heard a clicking of heels on the tiled floor of the reception area, and suddenly around the corner came this dapper little man in civilian clothes, accompanied by a uniformed policeman and police woman. They were being ushered towards us by the hotel manager. The police woman was carrying a bouquet of flowers nearly as big as herself. The little man bowed to us, and the police woman presented the bouquet of flowers to Sybil. They were representatives of the International Police Association and they were welcoming us to Italy.

The little man was ex-Chief of Police for the area. He later invited us to his home and took us on a sight-seeing tour in his car, which incidentally was quite frightening because, as he was driving, everytime he saw something that excited him, he would put both his hands up above his head and shout something in Italian. His hobby was taxidermy. In his home, there were glass cases filled with stuffed animals everywhere. It was more like a museum.

In September 1973, I went on my Home Office Police Dog Training Instructors Course at the Metropolitan Police Dog Training Establishment in Keston, Kent. It was an eight -week course and was very interesting. On the 2nd November, I was presented with my Instructor's Diploma by Mr Peter Matthews, Chief Constable of the Surrey Constabulary. I was to have many dealings with Mr Matthews in years to come, when he was the chairman of a Home Office Committee, of which I was to become a member.

In January 1974, I sat my Inspector's examination in Bristol and, on the 22nd March, heard that I had been successful in passing the exam. I was never one to be over ambitious, I was always happy with what I was doing at the time. But you see others doing things, and it gives you a bit of a jolt, and it makes you think, I could do that too.

Exactly two weeks later, an advert appeared in the Police Review for the post of Inspector in Charge of the Mounted and Dogs Section of the newly formed South Yorkshire Police.

I had seen the advert in the magazine in the afternoon, but I did not say anything to Sybil about it. Later that evening, when the girls had gone to bed, Sybil said to me, 'What do you think about that advert?' I pretended to look surprised and said, 'What advert?' She looked at me and said, 'You know what advert I mean.' Straight away, that told me that once again she was right behind me and was giving her support, if I was interested in the job. We talked it over that night and I decided that I would apply for the post. After informing my Chief Constable, I sent off my application.

I've always had plenty of confidence in my ability, and if I'd had any doubts whatsoever on whether or not I was capable of doing the job, I would never have applied for the post. Ever since joining the police force in 1959, I'd had plenty of experience working in close contact with others, and had very strong views on treating people in a manner that I wished to be treated myself. Man-management to me meant treating others at all times with respect, and being willing to consider the points of view of others, even if afterwards you didn't agree with them. I also enjoy a challenge, and I am a big believer in, 'nothing ventured, nothing gained.'

When all my colleagues at work were told of my decision, they were a little surprised, because they did not know anything about my previous experience with horses. On 20th May 1974, I had a letter from the Chief Constable of the South Yorkshire Police, informing me that I had been short-listed for the post, and asking me to attend at his headquarters in Sheffield on 23rd May for an interview. Once again, I felt the old butterflies in the stomach, but I believe that's a good sign.

The following Thursday, I travelled to Sheffield for my interview. Because I had not been to Sheffield before, and wanted to arrive in good time and not dishevelled, I went by train, which was my wife's idea. Going by train also gave me more time to relax and not to arrive tired. I arrived in Sheffield Railway Station in good time for the interview and walked the short distance to the South Yorkshire Police Headquarters, in Snig Hill.

On arrival at the Headquarters, I reported to Chief Superintendent Alan Robinson, head of the Personnel Department. I found him to be an extremely nice person, who immediately put me at ease. I sat in his office, which was in the old Headquarters building, as they were in the process of building a new headquarters, adjacent to the old premises, and it was only a few weeks from completion.

Shortly after my arrival, I was called in for my interview. It was with Mr Philip Knights, the Chief Constable, and Mr Bob Cozens, one of the Assistant Chief Constables. I felt quite relaxed and confident during the whole of the interview and answered various questions about my police service, particularly touching on my experience with horses and police dogs. At the conclusion of my interview, Mr Knights thanked me for coming to Sheffield and said that he had one more candidate to see, and that he would let me know the result of my application within a few days.

He then asked me if there was anything that I wished to say. I thanked them both for seeing me and said that I would be grateful if I could be informed of the result as soon as possible.

Mr Knights, who was never one to let anything pass said, 'Why is that?' I told him that I was living in my own house and that I was in the process of renovating the whole of the interior, all I had left to do was to wallpaper the hallway, stairs and landing. I went on the say that if I was successful with my application, I would be purchasing inexpensive wallpaper, but if I was unsuccessful, I would be purchasing more expensive paper. Mr Knights grinned, looked over at Mr Cozens and said, 'Mr Cozens, have we ever interviewed a more honest man?'

I left the room and returned to Chief Superintendent Robinson's office. As I entered his office, he grabbed hold of my arm, put me to sit in a chair behind the door, and said, 'Wait there', and was gone before I could say anything. I immediately thought that he had not realised that Mr Knights had finished with me. A couple of minutes later, he looked in around the door, and said, 'Things are going well', and was gone again before I could say a word.

About five minutes later, he came back and, not giving me a chance to say anything, quickly ushered me along the passage, saying 'Bryn, the Chief wants to see you again.' I tried to explain that the Chief had finished with me but, before I knew where I was, I was back in the Chief's office. Mr Knights and Mr Cozens were still sitting behind the large desk. Mr Knights looked up and said, 'I'm sorry to have messed you about like this, Mr Phillips, but things have moved a bit quicker than I anticipated. We have seen the last candidate, and we have decided to offer you the post of Officer in Charge of the South Yorkshire Police Mounted and Dogs Sections.' I told him that I would be pleased to accept the position and thanked them both.

Mr Knights shook hands with me, saying that Mr Cozens would deal with any domestic questions I may have and he left the room.

After Mr Cozens had dealt with me, I went back to Chief Superintendent Robinson's office. He said he was sorry for the confusion, but that he knew what was going on. He grabbed me by the hand, pointed to the telephone on his desk, and said 'Go on, ring the wife and tell her the good news.'

Having been told that I had been successful in my application for the post in Sheffield, we put our house in Bristol on the market. We were lucky, selling it to people who had just returned to this country from Australia, so there was no chain to hold things up at that end.

Towards the end of June, Sybil and I went to Sheffield, house-hunting. We fell in love with a little village called Grenoside, which is a couple of miles north of Sheffield on the Barnsley road. It was just about ten minutes in the car from where I'd be working. Not too near and in easy travelling distance. We saw a house in Grenoside that we both liked, and agreed to pay the asking price. On the Monday, when we returned to Bristol, I went to see my solicitor and gave him the name of the Estate Agent in Sheffield and told him to go ahead with the purchase of the house.

By then, I knew that I would be commencing my duties in Sheffield on 22nd July and that, until we had completed the purchase of the house in Grenoside, I was to be in lodgings in Hillsborough, pretty near to the Mounted and Dogs Headquarters at Niagra. In the meantime, I kept calling on my

89

solicitor in Bristol to see if they had heard anything from Sheffield on how the purchase of the house was progressing. Each time, I was told that they had heard nothing.

Fortunately, we had not yet fixed a completion date for the sale of our house in Bristol.

My last tour of duty with the Avon and Somerset Police, as it had become with amalgamation, was on the 8th July 1974. All the lads in the Mounted and Dogs Sections at Bower Ashton had given Sybil and I a lovely farewell party at the Bridewell Police Station Social Club. It was a lovely evening, but I don't like farewells.

On Sunday, 21st July 1974, I travelled to Sheffield in my nearly- new car, which I had bought from my dentist. It was a top of the range Ford. As I was travelling up on my own to commence my duties with the South Yorkshire Police, at least, I thought, it won't be long before Sybil and the girls will be joining me in our house in Grenoside. I arrived at my lodgings in Hillsborough about teatime and introduced myself to the family I'd be staying with. They made me very welcome, and, after tea, I told them that I was nipping up to Grenoside, about 10 minutes away, to call on the people whose house we were buying to see how things were progressing.

When I arrived at the house in Grenoside, I could see that there was someone at home through the glass front door, but it was ages before anyone answered to my knocking. Eventually, the lady of the house came to the door and looked very embarrassed to see me. When I asked her why we hadn't heard anything on how the transaction was progressing, she hesitantly said that she had decided to take the house off the market, but that she hadn't let the Estate Agent know for sure. I said, 'Thank you very much for having the decency to let us know,' and I walked away. I was so fed up, thinking of the delay that there would be now before Sybil and the girls could join me, that I immediately went to see another house in Grenoside and decided to buy it, even though Sybil hadn't seen it.

Next morning, 22nd July, I started my duties at the Mounted and Dogs Sections Headquarters at Niagra, which is about 10

90

minutes walk from the Sheffield Wednesday Football Ground, at Hillsborough. Until my arrival, there had been a Sergeant in charge of the Mounted Branch and a Sergeant in charge of the Dogs Section. I was to be the first Inspector in charge of both departments.

Although I had only ridden a horse a couple of times since I had horses of my own, I intended starting off as I meant to carry on. On my second day, Sheffield United Football Team were playing an evening home match at Bramall Lane, which is on the other side of the city to where the Mounted and Dogs Headquarters were based. We were covering the match with six horses that evening and, because our horse-box was off the road for repairs, it meant that the horses would have to be ridden to and from the ground, a distance of about four miles each way.

Although I did not have to, I had already decided that I would be one of the riders, and when we got back to the stables late that night, we had been in the saddle for over six hours.

Boy! did I suffer! I could hardly walk for a couple of days. Whilst it was not the reason why I did it, I know that it made an impression on the lads and they admired me for it, but at the same time I thought that I was bloody mad. I have never been one to ask anyone to do something that I wouldn't do myself. Riding a horse is no different to riding a bike, you never forget, it's all a matter of confidence.

For the next few weeks, I commuted between Bristol and Sheffield every weekend, and then we stayed with some friends in Finningley for a few weeks, until we moved into our house in Grenoside on 1st October 1974.

When we left Bristol, Marianne was in Training College there and she decided to stay on.

Apart from 12 months, when she came to live with us in Grenoside in 1975, she has lived in Bristol ever since. Lydia went to school in Wadsley Bridge, not far from where I worked, and Jeannette went to school in Ecclesfield, which is the next village to Grenoside. Sybil, who had been given a transfer, continued working part-time in Marks and Spencer, Sheffield.

Being that it was a new police force, there was obviously a lot of re-organising to do. During my first week, the Chief Constable sent for me. He welcomed me to the force and wished me luck for the future. He said, being a new force, things were at present a little disorganised. He asked me to have a good look around the force area, get to know my men, and then set out for him on paper how I thought that the Dog Section should be organised to the best advantage.

He said to take my time and let him have the report when I was ready.

The Mounted Section was no problem. They were all based at the same place, and the sergeant, John Pearson, could be relied on to run the stables efficiently. The Dog Section was a little different, as they were scattered all over the force area. We had dog handlers based at the three stations in the city, also at Hillsborough, Rotherham, Doncaster and Barnsley. There was a sergeant at each of these places and, over the next couple of weeks, we got together and, taking their views and experience in each area into consideration, I prepared a report on how I thought that the Dog Section should be organised to the benefit of the Section and the Force in general. It ensured proper and adequate coverage for the whole of the Force area. I submitted my report to the Chief Constable, which he agreed with, and the new ideas were put into operation. I had a busy time ahead of me, but I knew that I was going to enjoy it.

On 22nd September 1975, I started a 3-month Inspector's College Course at Hutton Hall, Preston. It was an interesting course which gave one an insight into many other organisations.

As well as attending lectures and having outside speakers on various subjects, we were sent out in groups to study the management, organisation, appraisal systems, etc. etc. of large firms and organisations. One of our visits was to Parkside Colliery, near Warrington. We were all issued with overalls and helmets and taken down the pit shaft and right up to the coal face to see the night- shift miners at work. From one of the underground roadways, we climbed up a ladder and then made our way right along the narrow coal face, where the miners were actually working. There was a huge machine grinding away at the coal, which was then being carried away on a conveyor belt. With the huge machine working at the coal, the coal dust was like a thick fog. As we made our way along the coal face, I clasped the hand of every miner I passed, if only to show my admiration for the work which they do. They are more than worth every penny that they earn. I must admit, I wouldn't work down there for a fortune.

I was also lucky to be in the group that went on a three-day visit to the Fire Service Technical College at Morton-on-Marsh. It was quite an experience to have a 'behind the scenes' view of a modern day Fire Fighter's training. I don't suppose that one can blame a lay person for thinking of a Fire Fighter as someone with a hose pipe, squirting water over a fire, but believe me, those days are long gone. The modern day Fire Fighter is a highly trained and skilled person. It is now a very technical job, which requires an in-depth knowledge of building structure, hazardous liquids, etc. etc.

We were shown all various techniques in dealing with different types of fires and accidents.

They had a huge model ship, which they could set alight to simulate an actual ship on fire, and buildings of all types, in which they could practise and train modern fire- fighting skills, and in which they could simulate any type of incident. It was a very interesting and informative three days. The Inspectors' Course finished on 12th December, and I returned to my normal duties. It had been an interesting three months, but I doubt very much that it had done anything to make me a better policeman.

A Police Mounted Branch, although very costly, can be a great asset to any police force. Many think that they are a luxury, but they show their true value when they are deployed at any outdoor event where there are large numbers of people involved. I can think of no better way in dealing with crowd control, one horse can do the work of very many men on foot. When police horses are engaged in crowd control, they do so in a passive manner and they are always accepted by the public. People are inclined to move out of the way of a horse and yet not feel put-out by having to do so.

A police officer on horseback has a great vantage point, and this is paramount when controlling large crowds of people or searching large areas of open ground for missing persons. When working amongst large crowds, mounted officers can see things happening that their colleagues on the ground cannot see. With this advantage, they can often deal with incidents before they get out of control.

Whilst stationed at Sheffield and Stafford, I performed regular mounted duties during the football season at the grounds of, Sheffield United, Sheffield Wednesday, Barnsley, Doncaster, Rotherham, Chesterfield, Derby, Stoke City, Port Vale and Stafford. We covered home matches at Derby, because Derbyshire Police did not have a Mounted Branch of their own. During the 1970's and 1980's, when football hooliganism was at its height, the use of police horses really came into its own. They saved many an ugly situation. I was on mounted duty at one evening match in Barnsley, when one of my police horses, Brigadier, lost an eye, when hit by half a brick thrown by a football hooligan. It was after the match and we were engaged in escorting spectators back to the coach station in the dark. The horse obviously had to be retired, and finished its life at a home for retired horses in Norfolk.

One Saturday in 1974, Manchester United , whose supporters had a very bad reputation in those days, were playing Sheffield Wednesday at Hillsborough. Hundreds , who had turned up for the match, failed to get into the ground and caused havoc outside the ground. We certainly had a busy afternoon. They turned dozens of cars onto their roofs, smashed the windows of all the coaches parked in a road near the ground, and caused damage to nearby houses and shops.

My wife, that afternoon, was travelling home by double decker bus from her work in Marks and Spencer, when hooligans outside the front of the ground, which was on the bus route, started rocking the bus, and tried to tip it over. With the police horses, we managed to clear the crowd away from the bus, for it to continue on its way. At the time of course I did not know that my wife had been one of the passengers. Even some of the supporters who had got into the match caused trouble

94

Bryn on police horse Brigadier at the Sheffield Wednesday -vs- Manchester United football match, 1974

Bryn on Police horse Brigadier, Bi–centennial parade at the St Leger meeting at Doncaster racecourse

and, at one stage, we had to take our horses on to the playing area to clear off fighting hooligans. I have purposely refrained from calling them fans, because that is not what they are.

Of course, apart from crowd control, police horses perform many other duties. Take Cannock Chase, in Staffordshire for instance. There are vast areas which are completely inaccessible to motor vehicles, because there are simply no roads. The only way to police the area properly is on horseback. This is an area which is frequented by thousands of people the year round, enjoying the lovely walks and views. The policeman on horseback is very much a traditional thing, going back to the beginning of many police forces. Although society has changed, and, along with it, its policing, I feel that there is still a need for horses in many police forces.

We also performed regular duty at Doncaster Race Course and on two occasions I led in the winner of the St Leger race. In 1975, Bruni, ridden by Tony Murray, and, in 1976, Crow, ridden by the French jockey, Yves St Martin. At the start of the 1976 St Leger meeting at Doncaster, on police horse Brigadier, I led a parade of six mounted police officers on the Race Course, each of us carrying the flag of each of the six nations taking part in the race, it being the bi-centennial St Leger Meeting.

Police horses also carry out street patrols in all towns in the Force area. The general public love to see the horses and riders on patrol in the streets, and its serves as a good public relations exercise.

When I was stationed at Stafford, my horses regularly competed in the Horse of the Year Show at Wembley, and at the Royal Tournament, Earls Court. Many may disagree, but exhibitions and competitions are an essential part of police horse work. They do not only compete for prestige, but it enables standards to be compared with other forces, and assesses horsemanship and training programmes. In 1983, Staffordshire Mounted Police won the highest number of trophies in the country. Winning the Police Horse Pairs Trophy at the Horse of the Year Show is among the highlights of the sections career.

97

When I first went to Sheffield in 1974, I was paying £400.00 to replace a police horse. During my last years in Stafford in the late 1980's, I was paying £2,000 plus to replace a horse.

Another sign of the times. We used to look for our horses to be at least 16 hands high and of good stock, preferably three-quarters bred. It takes anything up to eight months to train a police horse but, having said that, the training really continues for the rest of its service, in order to maintain the very high standard of efficiency and control required. It must be remembered that these horses are for much of the time, working in very close proximity to members of the public, and the temperament of the horse should be absolutely bomb-proof.

During my time in Sheffield, and because of my connection with police horses, I became friendly with a couple who owned several horses. One of their horses was called Storm and, although it was only 15,2 hands high, it was one of the bravest little horses I've ever seen. It was a terrific jumper and feared nothing. I became very attached to Storm and used to compete on him in Cross Country and Show Jumping events all over the county in my off duty time. I certainly missed riding him when I moved to Stafford.

When I became Inspector in Charge of the Mounted Branch of the South Yorkshire Police, I attended my first meeting of the National Mounted Conference, which was held annually at the British Equestrian Centre at Stoneleigh, Warwickshire. It was attended by senior mounted officers from all forces with Mounted Branches, and dealt with all matters appertaining to police horses. In 1979, when I was Chief Inspector in the Staffordshire Police, I was elected Secretary of the National Mounted Conference, a position I held for 5 years.

In August 1985, Rolls Royce, at their car plant in Crewe, held a. 'Cavalcade of the 100,000th Car.' One of the Managing Directors of the firm contacted our Chief Constable and requested if the Cavalcade could be led by Staffordshire Police Horses. The Chief Constable gave his approval and on the day I led the Cavalcade, riding police horse Chetwynd, with four other mounted officers flanking the lead car. The Cavalcade,

98

which had as the guest of honour, Mr Noel Edmunds, included every model of car made by Rolls Royce and made for a very spectacular showing. A few weeks before the Cavalcade, I had to go to Rolls Royce in Crewe to finalise details with the Managing Director involved. After the meeting, he took me out to lunch in a nearby village. After the meeting, when we went outside to go to lunch, there was a brand new top of the range Rolls Royce parked outside the door. The Managing Director opened the driver's door, looked at me and said, 'Come on Bryn, you don't think I'm going to drive you there as well.' I then had the pleasure of driving the car to the restaurant. What an experience! The disappointing part was, that he didn't tell me that I could keep the car.

In September 1976, an advert had appeared in the 'Police Review' inviting applications for the post of Chief Inspector in Charge of the Home Office Regional Police Dog Training School at Stafford, and the Staffordshire Police Mounted and Dogs Sections. The Dog School of course was where I had received my initial training as a dog handler. It was one of the prime posts in the country, as far as police dogs were concerned, and I must admit I did not hesitate in putting in my application.

On 1st November, I had a letter from the Chief Constable of the Staffordshire Police, informing me that I had been short listed for the post, and inviting me to attend at his headquarters for an interview on the 8th November. I was interviewed for the post by Mr Arthur Rees, the Chief Constable of the Staffordshire Police, and Mr Charles Kelly, the then Deputy Chief, who was later to succeed Mr Rees, on his retirement.

I must say that I have had better interviews and did not feel too confident when at the end Mr Rees told me that he had other candidates to see; he would let me know the result of my application at a later date. On the 11th November, I was at the British Equestrian Centre, Stoneleigh, attending a three-day Mounted Convention, when I had a telephone call from my wife, informing me that I had been successful in obtaining the post in Stafford. Sybil is not in the habit of opening my mail but, because the envelope had Staffordshire Police on it and she knew that I would want to know what it contained. She knew that I was to be promoted Chief Inspector before I did.

I knew that Sybil would be happy with the move as, although she never complained and we had many good friends in Yorkshire, I knew that she would be happier further south. In the December, we made a few visits to Stafford, house-hunting, and eventually bought a detached house at Weeping Cross, Stafford, within walking distance of the Police Headquarters where I was to be based. In the meantime, Sybil had been informed that she would be given an automatic transfer to Marks and Spencer in Stafford.

On the 21st December 1976, we were given a farewell party by all the lads on the Mounted and Dogs Sections. I'd been very happy in Sheffield and had learned a lot about the Mounted Police as, after all, I had never been trained to be a Mounted Police Officer but had learned the hard way, which I sometimes believe is the best way. In early January 1977, I had an interview with my Chief Constable, Mr Stanley Barratt, who had succeeded Mr Philip Knights. He thanked me for all that I had done for the South Yorkshire Police and wished me the best of luck and happiness in my new post at Stafford. He then said that he would like me to sit on the panel to choose my successor, and asked me to draw up a short list from the applicants. I thought that was a very nice gesture on his part and thanked him very much. My last working day with the South Yorkshire Police was on the 10th January 1977.

When I commenced my duties with the Staffordshire Police on the 29th January 1977, I knew that I had a very busy time ahead of me. My responsibilities were Director and Chief Instructor of the Home Office Police Dog Training School, and Officer in Charge of the Force Mounted and Dogs Sections.

Being that I was now Director of the Home Office Police Dog Training School, meant that I automatically became a member of the Home Office Standing Advisory Committee on Police Dogs (Training Sub Committee). I had been a judge at Regional Police Dog Trials since 1975, but now, as a member of the Home Office Committee, I became an Adjudicator at

Regional Police Dog Trials and a judge at National Police Dog Trials. Over the next ten years this took me to many different parts of the country, officiating at Police Dog Trials, and on many visits to Northern Ireland in connection with the training and use of Explosives Search Dogs.

In my new position at Stafford, I did not have a deputy. On the Regional Police Dog Training School, I had an admin' sergeant and later a secretary, three sergeant instructors, one of whom was on secondment from the West Midlands Police, and two constable instructors. On the Force Mounted Branch with 12 police horses, I had one sergeant and 14 constables. At that time, the Force Police Dog Section had 46 police dogs and handlers. They were based on Divisions, and I was responsible for the initial and continuation training of the handlers and the dogs.

All the dog handlers were supervised by the street patrol sergeants on their respective Divisions. We were about the only Police Force in the country that did not have operational sergeant police dog handlers. Whilst I mean no disrespect whatsoever to the street patrol sergeants, I felt that they did not have the necessary experience to supervise properly the operational police dog handlers. After all, they need specialist supervision in order to assess the deployment of the dogs, and to ensure that they are receiving adequate continuation training to maintain their standard of competence. I have never been one to claim that police dogs are indispensable, but like anything else, they have their limitations. Because they have become an operational part of the police service, then we should make sure that their standard of performance is kept at the level which is expected of them and that they are given every opportunity to perform the tasks for which they are originally trained. This can only be done by utilising properly their uses and ensuring that they receive the proper continuation training throughout their service.

On the Police Dog Training School at Stafford, each year we held 3 Initial Police Dog Training Courses (13 weeks duration) for police officers from this country and abroad, 3

Initial Prison Dog Training Courses (8 weeks duration) for prison officers and several Refresher Courses (2 weeks duration) for police officers and prison officers. In addition to these, we held 3 Specialist Courses (8 weeks duration) for drugs detection dogs and handlers, and explosives detection dogs and handlers, for police officers and prison officers from this country and abroad. The Police Dog Training School at Stafford has an excellent reputation. Over the years has been responsible for the training of handlers and dogs from many Police Forces in this country and abroad, and also handlers and dogs from, The British Army, The Prison Service, Central Electricity Generating Board, States of Jersey Police, Australia, Bahamas, Barbados, Bermuda, Ceylon, Chile, Jordan, Hong Kong, Lebanon, Malta, Nigeria, Seychelles, Sweden, Uganda, West Cameroons, St Lucia, Luxembourg, Tanzania, Lesotho, Ghana, Malawi, Bahrain, Cyprus, Jamaica, St Kitts, Mauritius, Oman and Pakistan. I am sure you will agree, quite an impressive record.

In 1979, the Police Dog Training School at Stafford was chosen by the BBC for an episode of *'It's a Dogs Life'*, portraying the training and work of police dogs. The programme was presented by Phil Drabble, who was also well known for 'One Man and his Dog' series. The film crew made their first visit to the school in April, at the start of a 13 week Initial Police Dog Handlers Course, and then made several visits throughout the Course, filming the progress of the handlers and the dogs. They also filmed an experienced dog handler on actual night patrol. The finished programme has been shown several times on BBC Television.

During my time as Director of the Home Office Police Dog Training School at Stafford, I lectured to ACPO Courses at Bramshill Police College on the use of police dogs in serious public order situations.

As a member of the Home Office Standing Advisory Committee on Police Dogs (Training Sub Committee) we dealt with matters appertaining to police dogs. The Training Sub-

Committee dealt mostly with matters concerning police dog training and police dog trials.

We would meet as a committee about five times a year, usually at the Headquarters of Sir Peter Matthews, the Chief Constable of the Surrey Constabulary, who was our chairman, and for my later years on the committee, at Aykley Heads, Durham, the Headquarters of Mr Boothby, the Chief Constable of the Durham Constabulary, who succeeded Sir Peter Matthews when he retired.

In 1984, a request was made by the authorities in Pakistan for a police dog expert to visit Pakistan to look at the existing training facilities at the Army Dog Centre in Rawalpindi and to advise on any further improvements there, with particular reference to establishing a drug-scenting facility, and to make further recommendations. The request was obviously passed on to the Home Office, and it eventually ended up with our committee.

I was fortunate and honoured to be the one sent on this assignment to Pakistan. When I was officially asked if I would be prepared to go to Pakistan on the assignment, I knew that it would be a challenge but I knew too that I had the confidence and the experience to carry it out.

All the arrangements for the visit were dealt with by the Overseas Development Administration. Prior to my visit, I had no information whatsoever on what to expect when I got there. I obviously thought that I would be dealing with the Pakistan Police and, at the time, did not know that it was the Pakistan Army that dealt with all the service dogs in Pakistan. As is usual with Government matters, it took some time for arrangements for the visit to be completed, but I was eventually informed that I would be going to Pakistan on 15th July 1984.

There were very few, if any, arrangements I could make prior to my leaving with regard to the actual visit, because I would be guided, obviously, by what I would find at the Army Dog Centre in Rawalpindi. I did not wish to have any preconceived ideas in case they did not fit in with what the Pakistani authorities had in mind. After all, I was to be their guest, and respecting their wishes was to be paramount in my objectives.

On the day that I left home for my visit to Pakistan, I was taken by police car to Birmingham Airport to catch the shuttle flight down to Heathrow. The shuttle was a twin-engine propeller aircraft with about 30-40 seats. It was only about half full and I had a window seat on the left-hand side of the plane. From where I was sitting I could see the propellers of both engines.

The left hand engine was a little way forward from the outside of the window where I sat. I could see the other engine by looking across to one of the windows on the right hand side of the plane.

We had an uneventful flight down and, when we were about 10 minutes out from Heathrow, on looking across to the right hand side of the plane, I noticed that the propeller of the right hand side engine had stopped. This did not cause me any alarm and, on looking around, it did not appear that anyone else had noticed this. I even thought that this might be normal procedure and that the pilot would re-start the engine on his approach to the runway. On the descent towards the runway I noticed that the plane was not flying level, but was tilting slightly to one side. As we touched down on the runway, there was a loud bang of a tyre bursting, and the plane slid off the runway onto the grass. As we came to a very bumpy halt, I could see that there were several fire-engines and tenders parked nearby. At first I thought how quick they had been in getting there, then it dawned on me that the pilot must have radioed ahead, warning that he had a problem and the emergency procedures had been put into action. There was no panic, but all the passengers were quickly taken off the plane and bused in to the terminal.

Tea was arranged for all the passengers, probably in the way of an apology, but I had to retrieve my baggage and book in for my onward flight BA223 to Islamabad with British Airways. We took off at 12.53pm in a Boeing 747 'City of Belfast'. I was flying at Super Club Class, in seat 59k on the upper deck. Shortly after take-off the Captain announced that we would be flying over France, Belgium, Germany, Turkey, Cyprus, Syria, Jordan, Saudi Arabia, and landing in Doha. At 4.30pm I visited the flight deck. At that time we were flying over Syria. The sky was cloudless and there was such a wonderful view of the Mediterranean down to our right. The Captain told me that we would be landing at Doha and Abu Dhabi, and then flying across the Indian Ocean, entering Pakistan just west of Karachi, and then flying up through Pakistan to Islamabad in the north.

At 6.45pm, as we were making the descent into Doha, the Captain announced that the temperature there was 100 degrees. It was now pitch dark, and what a wonderful sight it made with all the lights as we came in to land. It was announced that we could not leave the plane whilst in Doha, but I took a walk down on to the lower deck to stretch my legs. On looking out through one of the doorways, I could see a guard with a sub-machine gun standing at the bottom of each gangway. We took off from Doha at 8.06pm, and landed at Abu Dhabi 30 minutes later. There was a change of crew at Abu Dhabi, and some of the passengers disembarked. There were now only three passengers left on the upper deck. We took off from Abu Dhabi at 10.45pm and I settled down to try and get some sleep. At 2am (British time) we landed in Islamabad. It was of course, after 7am local time.

All planes at the airport in Islamabad come to a stop a long way from the terminal building and passengers have to be taken to the terminal in buses. I was quite some time retrieving my baggage, before making my way outside the airport buildings. I had no idea who was meeting me or where I was going to. I am not exaggerating when I say that there were several hundred people outside the building. It was pouring with rain, and the heat was unbelievable. For some minutes I stood looking at the sea of faces, not knowing what I was looking for. After a while, amongst the vast crowd, I saw a Pakistani man holding up a large card with Chief Inspector Phillips written on it. I introduced myself to him, and he took me to a British Embassy car in the Airport car park. The driver first took me to the Holiday Inn, where I would be staying, and then to the British Embassy. I had arrived, but what lay ahead? Your guess would have been as good as mine.

105

Staff at the Army training centre, Rawalpindi

Bryn with intructors and dog handlers
at the Army Dog Centre, Rawalpindi

106

At the Embassy, I was met by the Assistant Administration Officer, who welcomed me, and was then handed over to the Second Secretary. After a short talk, I was given 1060R advance subsistence and taken back to the Holiday Inn in the Embassy car.

I hadn't been back at the Holiday Inn long, when I was collected by a Colonel, who was the Deputy Director of the Army Dog Centre and taken to the Dog Centre in Rawalpindi. I had been told that, whilst there, I would be working, also, in close liaison with the Customs and Excise Authorities. At the Army Dog Centre, I was introduced to all members of the staff, who were all part of the Remount, Veterinary and Farms Corps., which is the equivalent of the Royal Veterinary Corps, in the British Army. Also present were the Investigating Officer, Narcotics Control, and Secretary Administration, Customs and Excise Control Board of Revenue.

We first had a long discussion on the training of dogs for narcotics detection, and then the Deputy Director gave a talk on the current work carried out at the Centre. I was then taken back to the hotel, after being told that I would be required again in the evening. At 5.15pm, I was again collected from the hotel and taken to the Dog Centre. On arrival, I was asked to supervise a demonstration by a group of handlers and dogs who were comparatively inexperienced, and to give my candid opinion on the performance. When the training session was in progress, The Director of the Army Dog Centre, who was a Major General, arrived and, after being introduced to me, sat down beside me.

During my conversation with the Director, he asked me if I would fly down to Karachi Airport on the Wednesday, so that I could assess the drugs searching dogs that were based at the airport. The dogs and handlers had been trained in Germany. At 8.30pm that evening, I was taken back to the Holiday Inn in Islamabad, after being told that I would be collected from the hotel at 6am next morning. During the rest of my visit, I was to have a Customs and Excise Staff car and driver at my disposal.

The next morning, 6am on the dot, I was picked up by a uniformed driver from the Customs and Excise Control Board and taken to the Dog Training Centre at Rawalpindi. The journey from the Holiday Inn in Islamabad to the Dog Training Centre in Rawalpindi, takes about 45 minutes. We drove the whole of the journey through torrential rain, the like of which I had never seen before. The roads were flooded to such an extent that I don't know-how we completed the journey.

The Army Dog Training Centre was a very impressive establishment with really attractive grounds and an excellent Kennels complex. At that time, they were, in fact, building another kennel complex, adjacent to the existing one, to increase the training facilities. That morning, we travelled to a hilly area some 10 miles away to observe a group of handlers and dogs going through various stages of tracking training. Again, I was asked to give my opinion on the methods being used and to point out any faults in the training methods. This I did in my usual candid manner.

On our return to the Dog Training Centre, I had a long discussion with all the training staff on all aspects of training dogs for tracking, and explained methods which would be much quicker and produce better results than what they were now having. At 2pm I returned to the Holiday Inn, where I had a meeting with the Chairman, Central Board of Revenue, and Chairman of the Narcotics Board and others of their staff. We discussed in length the training and use of dogs for narcotics detection.

On the Wednesday, I was picked up from the hotel at 7am by my driver and taken to the Army Dog Training Centre.

Together with members of the training staff, who incidentally were all of the ranks of Captains, Majors and Colonels, we travelled to an area to watch handlers and dogs carrying out criminal work training, and for me, once again, to give my candid opinion on what I saw. I thought that a lot of what they did was totally unnecessary and I explained to them a more effective method which would get better results.

Back at the Training Centre, I was thanked by the Deputy Director for the forthright way in which I had expressed my opinion on all that I had seen. He went on to say that he had learned much in a few days and that he was looking forward very much to the overall report on my visit and the future of the Army Dog Training Centre.

When I was taken back to the Holiday Inn at lunch time, I had a swim in the hotel pool before having my lunch. At 3pm, my driver collected me from the hotel and took me to the airport for my flight down to Karachi. At the airport, I was met by the Deputy Customs Controller of the Airport and the Public Relations Officer, Customs Control, in the VIP Lounge. One of the staff was sent to collect my boarding card, and I was then taken by the Deputy Controller and his Superintendent in their staff car out to the aircraft, a Boeing 747, which I boarded at 6.15pm.

We had been told earlier that the take-off time had been delayed for some reason. Shortly after boarding, the Captain announced that take-off was being further delayed because they were experiencing very extreme storms over Karachi, and conditions were far too bad for landing.

Just then, the air-conditioning system of the plane cut out. All the doors of the plane had been closed, and the heat became unbearable, with the plane full to capacity. Babies started crying, and some of the women passengers became hysterical. After some arguing between some of the passengers and members of the cabin crew, the doors were opened, which gave a little relief. Two maintenance vehicles came out and there was a lot of activity underneath the plane. Two hours and twenty- five minutes late, the plane took off for Karachi.

After about 20 minutes flying, it was pitch dark. Once the sun goes down in Pakistan, it gets dark almost immediately. Half way down to Karachi, we ran into a violent electric storm, the like of which I had never seen. The lightning, which was constant, could be heard sizzling as it hit the plane, and the turbulence was tossing the plane around like a kite, despite its size. It was one time that I was glad that Sybil wasn't with me. I had a window seat and enjoyed seeing it all.

We touched down in Karachi Airport at 9.05pm in very heavy rain. I was later told that our plane was the only one to land at the airport that day, because of the extreme weather conditions they'd been having. Incidentally, the Director of the Army Dog Centre, who had flown down on an earlier flight to meet me at the airport, had to return to Islamabad because the plane could not land, owing to the bad conditions.

I was met at the airport terminal by Customs and Excise Officers, and introduced to the Army Major, who was in charge of the handlers and drugs detection dogs based at the Airport.

After a brief talk, I was taken by staff car into the city, where I had been booked into the Holiday Inn. The driver said that it was the first rain they had had for eleven months.

I had a meal in the hotel restaurant, which I finished off with a peach melba and, after writing up my report for the day, went to bed. I woke up in the middle of the night with terrible stomach pains, and regretted having that peach melba.

Next morning, I got up about 8am and decided that I would go for a short walk, as I was not being picked up until 10am. When I stepped outside the hotel door, it was like walking in to a sauna. The heat and the humidity was unbearable. I'd only been out for about 15 minutes and my shirt was soaking wet. The humidity was much worse than up in the north of the country.

At 10am, I was collected from the hotel by the Major, who took me to meet a Lt. Colonel from the R. V. F. C., Karachi Headquarters, and we then went to Karachi Airport. At the airport I was met by the Assistant Controller of Customs, Karachi Airport, the Assistant Controller from Customs House, Karachi, the Superintendent in Charge of Drugs Enforcement Cell and other officers of the Customs and Excise. They were certainly taking my visit very seriously.

I then accompanied them all out to where the baggage for the next outward flight was being loaded into containers, to watch two trained drugs detection dogs and handlers search the baggage for any illegal drugs. I was asked to give my candid opinion of what I thought of the dogs' performance and the way they were worked by the handlers. I had a long discussion with all present on the way which the dogs were worked and what I thought of their performance.

After the discussion I was taken to Customs House, in the Port of Karachi to meet the Controller of Customs (Preventive), who was obviously a very important man. After taking tea with him and his staff, we had a very long discussion on the future of Drugs Detection Dogs in Pakistan.

After lunch, I was taken into the city by the Major on a short shopping trip and to see some of the sights. I found Karachi to be really fascinating, with camels drawing large carts, and snake charmers in the streets. When we got back to Karachi Airport, I was asked to inspect the kennels and quarters of the drugs dogs and handlers. Before leaving Karachi, I was given tea in the V. I. P. lounge and then escorted out to the plane by a high ranking officer, after saying my good-byes to everyone. I must say that they had taken a tremendous interest in my visit and had shown the utmost concern and respect in what I had discussed with them.

I had a very pleasant flight back to Islamabad, made more interesting by a 9 year old Pakistani boy who was sitting next to me on the plane. He was a good looking lad, very talkative and obviously intelligent. He told me that all his family were on board, sitting two rows in front of us. We talked for the whole of the flight about all sorts of things. His English was excellent, but then, it's the first language of a lot of people in Pakistan. He said that his father was a Bank Official and worked in Islamabad. He seemed so interested when I told him about my working with dogs, and he said that I was to be his new friend. When we landed at Islamabad Airport, I was met at the bottom of the gangway by a group of Customs and Excise Officers and taken to a nearby staff car. Before moving off, I could see the little boy, who was now with his father, pointing towards me and obviously telling him of his meeting with me. We waved to each other until the car drove away and out of his view. I thought at

111

the time, how wonderful it would be if all nationalities of the world could forge such friendships. What a better world it would be to live in.

Back at the terminal, I had tea in the V. I. P. lounge with the Customs Officials and, after saying my good-byes, I was taken by my driver back to the Holiday Inn. I had a bath and, after writing up my report for the day, went to bed as I was not feeling too good. I had only been in bed about 10 minutes, when I suddenly went very cold and started shivering violently - then I started to sweat profusely. There was not much that I could do about it, as there was no-one that I could turn to. I did not sleep all night, but just lay in bed waiting for the morning.

I got up and showered about 7am and, half an hour later, was picked up by my driver and taken to the Army Dog Centre. By then, I was feeling a little better, but very weak on my feet.

I felt sure that it was due to the peach melba that I had eaten in Karachi.

At the Dog Centre, they were all patiently waiting for me. They all, I'm sure, appreciated me being there, and were very eager to learn as much as they could about dog training. We all went out to an area about ten miles from the Centre for me to see another demonstration on how they train their dogs to track. They were amazed when I told them that back in the UK, we would expect dogs to be performing good tracks after about 3 to 4 weeks of training. I then gave them a demonstration with an untrained dog, on how to teach a dog to perform a simple track in a matter of minutes. They could hardly believe what they saw. Back at the Dog Centre, I gave a long talk on the 'properties' and 'formulation' of scent, and it really raised their enthusiasm. The Director then asked me if the next day, because it would be my last at the Dog Centre, if I would give a comprehensive talk to all the staff, touching on all aspects of dog training that we had done during the week. All the staff were ordered to attend, even if it was their day off.

After the talk, the Deputy Director took me to his house to meet his wife and some of his family. The house, which belonged to the Pakistan Army, had been originally built by the British

Army when they were in Pakistan. The Colonel usually lived there on his own, as his permanent home was in Lahore. His wife and children, of course, came to live with him when the children were on holiday from school. His sister-in-law and her children were also staying there at the time. Her husband was also a Colonel in the Pakistan Army. I was given tea and cakes, along with his children who seemed to enjoy meeting me. The Colonel commented on this.

After tea, I was taken back to my hotel in Islamabad, where I watched a couple of films on television in my room. At about 10pm I asked the Hotel Telephone Operator to book me a call to the UK, for any time that my wife could get through. Later, I was half asleep when the telephone rang. It was Sybil, and it was so good to hear her voice. I told her that it was less than 48 hours now, and I'd be home.

On the Saturday morning, my last working day in Pakistan, I woke at 6.30am by the house-boy bringing me breakfast. I thought that I would spoil myself on my last day. After breakfast, I was picked up by my driver and taken to the Army Dog Centre. They were all there waiting for me, eager to get started. I commenced my talk at 8.15am and carried on non-stop until 10.50am and then answered questions for twenty minutes. The Director and all staff were present, with everybody taking notes. We then had tea, sandwiches and cakes and I was then given a demonstration by a group of handlers and dogs of some of the things they had learned during the week.

After the demonstration, we all went back into the Lecture Room, where the Director gave a speech of thanks for all that I had done for them during the week. He said that he had been connected with the Dog Training Centre since it's inception in 1952, but that he had learned more from me during the week, than in all the time before. Then, on behalf of himself and all the staff he presented me with a lovely plaque of the Remount, Veterinary and Farms Corps, and also a present of a sari for my wife. In response, I thanked him for his very kind words, and everyone present for the gifts, and I went on to say that I had already been rewarded enough by their sincere enthusiasm, willingness to learn, and the way in which they had all accepted my constructive criticism. I added that I was sure that their attitude and enthusiasm would ensure their future success.

The Major General then took me in his staff car to see the new kennel complex, accommodation and administration block, that was being built nearby. On returning to the Dog Training Centre, I had my photograph taken with all the staff. My driver was then summoned to take me back to the hotel but before we left the Major General issued instructions that the staff car was to be put at my disposal for the rest of the day, and a Colonel was to accompany me on a sight-seeing trip. I then said my good-byes to all the staff. At 1.30pm my driver dropped me off at the Holiday Inn, saying that he would collect me at 7.30am next morning to take me to the airport.

The Colonel and his driver picked me up from the hotel at 2.30pm and we drove up into the Muree Hills. We first called at Muree, where I took some photographs, and then continued up into the hills (we would have called them mountains). That afternoon, I saw some sights and scenery that I would always remember. Right up in the hills, which are the foothills of the Himalayas, it was like being in another world.

The Colonel took me to see his 'Rest Home', near one of the Army Farms. It was what we would call a holiday home, where he took his family for holidays. The Army Farms, which they have all over the country, are owned by the Army, but are run by civilians. When we were at the Colonel's holiday home, some of the men from the nearby farm came to make tea for us. It was good to talk to them, and some of them remembered the British Army, when they were in Pakistan. I found them to be very pro-British. We stayed at the house for about an hour, having our tea out on the lawn, believe me, way up in the clouds. As we drove back down the mountain roads towards Islamabad, the scenic views were unbelievable.

We arrived back at the Holiday Inn at about 8.30pm. I thanked the Colonel for a really wonderful day and he said that he would be at the airport to see me off in the morning. I went to my room to finish my packing. I felt that I had enjoyed the week immensely, but I would be happy to get home. Next morning, the Colonel was at the airport to see me off. I boarded my plane, a Pakistan International Airlines, Boeing 747, at 10,55am local time, and we took off, 1 hour and 10 minutes late. We landed in Tehran at 10.10am. British Time. As we came in to land, I could see painted in large letters on the side of one of the airport buildings, DOWN WITH THE USA. I was rather surprised that we had landed in Tehran but, of course, British planes did not land there. We took off from Tehran at 11.45am, and landed at Heathrow at 6.10pm. I caught the shuttle to Birmingham and touched down at 8.16pm. Sybil, my daughters Marianne and Lydia, my grandchildren Neil and Leanne and my mother-in-law, were there meeting me. It was great to be home.

When I returned from my assignment to Pakistan, I submitted a comprehensive report of my findings to the Government, setting out full details of the existing facilities at the Army Dog Training Centre at Rawalpindi, and the level of dog training knowledge which they had at the Centre at the present time. I candidly pointed out that their lack of knowledge of modern methods of training dogs were not conducive with improving the dogs' present standard of competence. Whilst all the staff at the Dog Training Centre were fluent in English, this was not so with the dog handlers, most of whom couldn't speak a word of English. For this reason alone, I did not think it practical for the dog handlers to come to England to attend Dog Handlers Training Courses. I felt that it would be far more expedient for the Instructors to come to this country for training, or, far less costly, for an experienced Instructor from this country to go to Pakistan to train all the Instructors in the Pakistan Army. They would then, obviously, be qualified to train their own dog handlers.

Dogs, whilst they very much lack human intelligence, are extremely perceptive and communicate mostly by body language. Because of this, if an Instructor had to train a dog handler, who did not understand his language, but had to receive all his instructions through an interpreter, the whole concept

115

would be lost to the dog. It would be totally impracticable, and would only end up in confusing the dog.

I had been sent to Pakistan to look at the existing facilities and to advise on further improvements, with particular reference to drugs detection, and to make further recommendations. Taking full regard of what I had seen during my visit, I felt that the only conclusions I could reach were the recommendations that I had made in my report. I must say here that, when I was in Pakistan, telling them of the methods of training that we used in this country with so much success, I was always aware of the fact that one day I might have to put my money where my mouth was. By this, I mean that I knew that it was more than a possibility that I'd be asked to be the one to go to Pakistan to carry out these methods of training, if my recommendations were accepted. This did not deter me in any way, as I knew that the methods of training that we used at the Dog Training School at Stafford were highly successful.

After I'd submitted my report to the Overseas Development Administration, I knew that it would take some time before any final decision would be made regarding my findings and recommendations.

116

CHAPTER EIGHT
THE PROOF OF THE PUDDING ...

A few months after I had submitted my comprehensive report on my findings at the Army Dog Centre, Rawalpindi, as I had anticipated, it became evident that I was to be asked to return to Pakistan to put into practice all the recommendations that I had made after my initial assignment. It obviously took some time for arrangements to be finalised between the two governments. It was eventually decided that I should return to Pakistan in September 1985. This gave me ample time to work out in my mind how I was going to put into operation a completely new dog training programme in the Pakistan Army, and I was determined that it was going to be successful. At that time I had over 20 years experience as an operational dog handler and dog training instructor, including specialist training in drugs and explosives detection. As well as having a wealth of experience, I knew from my first visit that I would have all the co-operation necessary from the Pakistan Army authorities. I had already witnessed their enthusiasm and eagerness to learn, and knew that this would be a bonus. As the time for my assignment drew nearer, I felt my own enthusiasm increase, and I was determined that this was a challenge that I was not going to miss.

On the 28th September 1985 I left home for my second visit to Pakistan, knowing that I now had to put into practice all the claims that I had made the previous year, of what the modern methods of dog training could achieve. Once again, the start of my journey was a little eventful.

I was taken to Birmingham by police car driven by one of my mounted officers, John Matthews, to catch the shuttle flight down to Heathrow Airport. On arrival at Birmingham we found the Airport to be completely fog-bound, with all inward and outward flights delayed.

I was advised by the Airport authorities to make my own way to Heathrow in order to catch my connecting flight to Islamabad. I contacted the Police Control Room at Stafford and was given permission for the police car to take me on to Heathrow. We arrived at Heathrow Airport at 10am, and found the same predicament there, thick fog delaying all flights. My Pakistan International Airlines flight, PK 786, was fog- bound in Copenhagen and it was not known what time it would be arriving at Heathrow. The whole of the Airport was in complete disarray, with thousands of passengers, many of whom had been waiting for hours for their flights. After a struggle through the crowded terminal, I managed to make my way to the PIA desk, and booked in my baggage and received my boarding card. I was told to watch the display screens for any further information.

At 12.10pm the screen showed that my flight was delayed until at least 2pm. At 2.05pm we were called to the Boarding Lounge and boarded the plane at 2.40pm. We took off at 3.45pm, three and a half hours late, but sooner than I had expected in the conditions. I had a window seat on the top deck of the Boeing 747. Shortly after take-off the Captain announced that we were to land in Paris. When we took-off from Paris, the Captain announced that we would be flying over France, Germany, Czechoslovakia, Poland and Russia, and into Northern Pakistan - obviously a completely different route to that of British Airways flights.

It was about 7am Pakistani time, when we arrived over Islamabad Airport and, for some reason, had to circle a couple of times before making our final approach, then landed to a lovely sunny morning. After collecting my baggage and making my way through immigration, I arrived outside the terminal building in the stifling heat to face a crowd of hundreds who were meeting passengers off the plane.

I had no idea who I was to meet and, after scanning the sea of faces for several minutes, saw a Pakistani man holding up a placard with 'Chief Inspector Phillips' written on it. I made my way towards him , and he took my bags and led me to a British Embassy car. We then drove along the familiar route to the Holiday Inn, where I had stayed on my first visit. At the hotel, I checked in and went to my room, No.404. I hadn't been in my room many minutes when the telephone rang. It was the British

Embassy, and arrangements were made for me to be collected from the hotel at 11.15am and taken to the Embassy. Shortly afterwards, the telephone rang again, and it was the Major from the Army Dog Centre in Rawalpindi, wanting to know what time I would be arriving at the Dog Centre. I informed him that I would come as soon as I had been to the British Embassy, and, at the same time, thinking, 'They don't intend wasting any time.' To me, this was very pleasing, as it was indicative of the keenness and enthusiasm that they had shown on my first visit. I felt that it was good to work with people who were so willing to learn from the experience of others.

I arrived at the British Embassy at 11.40am and was met by the Second Secretary (Aid) and T. C. O. (Admin'). After a short conversation on the reason for my visit, arrangements were made for a hired car from the Holiday Inn to take me to the Army Dog Centre at Rawalpindi.

At the Dog Centre, I had a very enthusiastic welcome from Major Chaugtai, the Officer in Charge of the Centre. I showed him a copy of my contract, and he made several telephone calls to sort out my future travelling arrangements. This was soon resolved by an Army Staff car and driver being put at my disposal, from the next day, for the duration of my stay.

Major Chaugtai then introduced me to all the Instructors who would be involved in the training programme. They were Major Iftifhar Ahmad Khan, Major Maqbool Hussain Kauser, Capt. Muhammad Asghar, Capt. Muhammad Ali Asghar Raza and Capt. Muhammad Afzal Raza. They were all members of the Remount, Veterinary and Farms Corps of the Pakistan Army and qualified veterinary surgeons. They were a very friendly and enthusiastic bunch of chaps, and made no secret of how much they were looking forward to working with me. Their attitude immediately made me feel at home in their company, and I felt that the visit was going to be a big success. In the lecture room, I gave an introductory talk on what the training programme was going to consist of and what I expected of them. I could tell from their general attitude that I was going to enjoy the assignment.

119

Early afternoon I was conveyed back to the Holiday Inn in the hired car. Incidentally, during my time in Pakistan, I was paid subsistence by the British Embassy every week, which I had to collect and settle all my bills, including my hotel account. The next morning I was collected from the hotel at 6.30am by the Army staff car and driver and taken to the Army Dog Centre.

On arrival at the Centre, I first had a short discussion with all the Instructors, and was then taken to see all the equipment that I had requested for use on the training course, e.g., firearms, various explosives materials and various types of narcotics. I found it all to be adequate and suitable for the training programme which lay ahead.

I was then taken to meet all the dog handlers who would be attending the course. They were all novice handlers, none of whom spoke English. This meant that all my instructions would have to be translated to the handlers by the Instructors, all of whom spoke fluent English. All the handlers, each with his own dog, were then divided into four groups of five, with an Instructor in charge of each group, and one extra Instructor. Each of the Instructors also had a dog to handle and train.

Of course, the main object of my visit was to impart my experience and knowledge of dog training methods to the Instructors. By doing this, they would then be sufficiently qualified to pass on their expertise to future courses held at the Army Dog Centre. The four groups consisted of: Firearms/Explosives Detection Training - Narcotics Detection Training - Guard Dog Training - Tracking Training. All the dogs in the Guard Dog and Tracking groups were German Shepherds. The dogs in the Specialist Search groups were a mixture of Labrador's and German Shepherds. None of the dogs, all of which had been bred at the Centre, had as yet received any training.

Via the Instructors, I impressed on all the handlers the utmost importance of the rapport which must exist between handler and dog in order to get the best results. I then issued each handler and Instructor with an 8-inch long piece of rubber hose pipe,

120

and explained to them the importance of each of them getting their dog to play with and retrieve the article. I told them that the reason for this would become evident later in the training.

Afterwards, in the Lecture Room, I discussed with the Instructors the training programme for the first week. I asked them to impress upon all the handlers the importance of a good relationship being built up between each man and his dog. Also, that all success achieved by the dog should be rewarded with praise, stressing the point that the opposite of reward was not punishment, but absence of reward. Because all of the dogs had been bred at the Dog Centre and had had little or no contact with people, they did not possess the usual confidence and personality generally found in dogs of that age. Because of this, I knew that I would have to be extra careful when introducing them to the more serious training.

At 1pm I was conveyed back to the Holiday Inn by my driver, as it was far too hot to work the dogs in the afternoons. After lunch, I spent the afternoon in and by the hotel swimming pool. Also enjoying the pool were some of the crew of a British Airways Boeing 747, who were staying the night at the hotel. They invited me to join them that evening. Later, I enjoyed meeting all the crew for a drink in the Captain's room, and then we all went for a meal together. I was quite surprised that they did not know each other and had only flown together for the first time on that particular flight. They were returning to the UK early the next morning. I very much enjoyed their company and found them a very friendly group.

I was at the Dog Centre by 7am the following morning so that we could make an early start and get much of the work done before it got too hot. First, I supervised the dog handlers and the Instructors with their dogs in a session of basic obedience. As to be expected with novice handlers, they were making many mistakes, but correcting them at this early stage meant there was less chance of them becoming confused. It is especially important with dog training that mistakes and handling faults are corrected from the beginning, so as to prevent the handlers and dogs developing bad habits.

Later that morning, I gave the Instructors a talk on 'Introduction to searching', and followed this up with a long discussion on the morning's work. I certainly did not want to rush things, but wanted to make sure that everything was fully understood, before moving on to the next stage. During my talk in the Lecture Room, I had noticed a gentleman in civilian clothes sitting in and showing great interest in what I was saying. During the talk he asked many interesting questions. I naturally thought that he was another Army Officer, perhaps off duty. Early that afternoon, having returned to the Holiday Inn, I was relaxing in my room, when I had a telephone call from the front desk, informing me that I had a visitor in reception. On going down to the reception area, I found the visitor to be the gentleman who had sat in on my morning's talk.

He introduced himself to me as Anwar Husain. He was a local business man, and was Secretary of the Pakistan Kennel Club. We had a very long interesting talk on dogs and, before leaving, he said that he would return later and take me out for a meal. Later, Anwar collected me from the hotel and took me to a local restaurant for a lovely meal. After the meal, Anwar took me to his home on the outskirts of Islamabad to meet his wife, Najma. At his home, Anwar had seven German Shepherds and was obviously very dog- orientated. He took me back to the hotel later that evening and, as he left, I knew that I had made a very good friend.

I rang the switchboard and booked a telephone call to the UK. At 10.55pm the telephone rang, and it was Sybil on the line. It was so good to hear her voice, and ended off for me a very lovely day.

Next morning at the Dog Centre, I again concentrated on basic obedience, as I always consider this to be a sound foundation for success in any form of dog training. When a dog is obedient it is more likely to pay attention to what commands you are giving it. I closely watched all the handlers with their dogs, at the same time giving them advice on correction of basic faults in leash handling, commands to the dog, inducements, positioning of dog, understanding the reason for dog's faults,

122

etc. etc. At first it was a little difficult, as with the language problem, much of the effect of instant correction was lost, due to my advice having to be translated to the handlers via the Instructors. Fortunately, this soon sorted itself out, and much progress was made in the first few days.

With the constant handling and mixing with people, all the dogs were now beginning to show more confidence and were re-acting in the manner that they should for their age. On the Wednesday morning, I had all the Instructors to give a ten minute lecturette each on a subject chosen by myself. All the subjects related to matters that I had covered in my talks. The results were good, which to me, indicated that they had been taking in what I had been telling them.

I had been asked by Anwar if I would be prepared to start dog training sessions for civilian dog owners in Islamabad, with a view to them starting a Dog Training Club. I considered it an honour to be asked and readily said that I would be delighted to do so.

At about 5pm on the Wednesday, Anwar picked me up from the hotel and took me to a local park, where there were about eight people waiting for us with their dogs. Anwar introduced me to the group and explained who I was and that I was going to give them some instruction in dog training. As they all spoke English, I first gave them a short talk on the principles of basic obedience, and then gave them a demonstration with one of the dogs on how to walk correctly a dog on a leash without interfering with the dog's movements. I then had them all joining in a session of practical obedience with their dogs and, considering their inexperience, was delighted with the results. I was also very impressed with their enthusiasm. Before leaving, it was arranged that I would give regular training sessions during my stay in Pakistan.

After the training session, Anwar took me to his home, where we had cold drinks, and he then took me on a tour of the city, showing me all the Embassies and Government buildings. Later in the evening he took me to meet some friends of his, Eve and her daughter Marie Jo. Eve was French, but had been brought

123

up in England and was very British in her ways. Her husband, another Anwar, was a retired Airline Pilot, and had a farm down in Karachi. He was away on the farm at the time, so I did not meet him until later. Eve had a lovely German Shepherd dog called Shane, and when she and Marie Jo heard that I had started dog training classes, they were very interested and immediately expressed their desire to join.

When Anwar took me back to the hotel that evening, he said that on Friday, which was my day off, he was going to take me on a trip up into the foothills.

On the Thursday, I saw a vast improvement in the way which all members of the course were handling their dogs, which was very encouraging. They were obviously taking in all that I was telling them and putting it into practice. So far, we concentrated solely on obedience, because I wanted a good rapport established between the handlers and their dogs before starting the more serious training.

At 11.30am that day, I had a telephone call from Kerry Hill at the Australian Embassy, inviting me to join them at the Embassy that afternoon. He said that an Embassy car would pick me up at the Holiday Inn. Sure enough, at 3pm, an Australian Embassy car picked me up at the hotel, and took me out to their Embassy, where I met Kerry Hill, a Police Detective Inspector, who was First Secretary at the Embassy, Kevin Byron, an official at the Embassy, Norbert Pehlke, a police officer from the German Embassy, and Ollie, from the Norwegian Embassy. They all made me so welcome and we had a lovely afternoon of conversation. I had a job convincing Kerry that I wasn't a Rugby fanatic, despite being Welsh.

It gives me no pleasure in mentioning here, that I had no such hospitality from the British Embassy the whole time that I was in Pakistan. Not once did they contact me to inquire into how my official business was progressing, nor as to my welfare.

At 5.30pm I was taken back to the hotel, and at 6.45pm was again picked up by Anwar and his wife, and taken to the home of Kevin Byron and his wife, Megan, where we had a lovely meal.

Also present were two other Australians, Gregg and Helen. We all had a very enjoyable evening. Before dropping me off at the hotel later that evening, Anwar said that he would be collecting me at 8am next day for our trip up to the foothills.

Next morning, together with Anwar and Najma, their friends Jamal Raja and his American wife, Anilea, we travelled up to the foothills to Ayubia District, Khanspur (meaning inhabited by Khans), which is in the North West Territory.

Up in the foothills (mountains to us), was like being in another world. The views and scenery were breathtaking, and I was able to take some lovely photographs. There were precarious houses on ledges carved out of the treacherous slopes of the hills. They were linked by a fragile web of precipitous footpaths, with little pieces of terraced ground to produce crops.

Many of the people living there had never been away from the immediate area in their lives.

We visited Jamal's summer cottage, which years ago was one of the buildings built by the British Army. Nearby, I met a very old man, who was very proud to tell me that he used to work for the British Army. The way that he stood erect as he told me, I could see that the memories meant a lot to him. He shook my hand and and was half reluctant to let go. It was a day and place that I will never forget.

It was dark when we began our journey back down to Islamabad. The journey down the unmade mountain roads was like something one sees in the films. At one point, we were stopped by a tree-trunk barrier across the road and a group of fierce looking tribesmen. They started questioning Anwar, asking if I was British and whether I was a Christian. When Anwar told them that I was working for the Pakistan Army, they quickly raised the barrier and signalled us through.

When I got back to the hotel, there were two messages in reception for me. One was from Norbert, saying that he had called to see me, and the other was a letter from Brian Watkins, a First Secretary at the British Embassy, inviting me to dinner at his home on Sunday evening.

He said in his letter that he was Welsh, and that they had some friends from Wales staying with them. It was a pleasant surprise and gave me something to look forward to. It was, of course, a private invitation, he had nothing to do with my official business in Pakistan. At 9.15pm, I had a crate of beer delivered to my room from the German Embassy. I knew of course that was Norbert's doing.

On the Saturday morning, we drove to the Army Dog Centre in torrential rain and constant thunder and lightning. When we arrived, because of the weather, I decided that we would begin the day with a lecture for the Instructors on 'Selection of dogs for searching' and 'Search techniques'.

By about 11am the weather had improved and, on grassland near the Centre, we commenced tracking training. Before any attempt is made to teach a dog to track, it is of the utmost importance that everyone concerned in the training, i.e., dog handlers, track-layers and Instructors, should know that it is essential that the dog is introduced to this form of training in the proper manner. All future progress by the dog is dependant on the amount of care and planning put into every stage of training.

I first laid a one leg track, which means that I walked out in a straight line for about 30-40 yards, with the handler and dog watching. At the end of the straight line, I placed an article, which the dog was familiar with, on the ground and then returned to where the handler and dog was by a different route, making sure that I was down wind of the line at which I had walked out, so as not to interfere with it. A tracking harness and line was then put on the dog and the dog was encouraged to put it's nose down and follow the scent left on the ground where I had first walked out in a straight line. As training progresses, each turn or change of direction from the initial straight line, adds another leg to the track. Also, the time lapse between the laying of the track and the dog being put to follow the scent is increased.

I was more than pleased with the initial results. All the dogs performed the one leg track which was five minutes old without any difficulty. Later in the morning we had our first session with

126

the search dogs. Since the start of the training course, all the handlers had been practising the retrieve with their dogs, using the piece of hose-pipe I had issued them with on the first day. Now, I stuffed cotton wool, impregnated with the smell of cannabis, into the pieces of hose-pipe for the drugs search dogs, and cotton wool impregnated with the smell of explosives; for the explosives search dogs, I then had the handlers to do several retrieves with the impregnated articles. Later, hiding the article out of the sight of the dog and then commanding the dog to 'seek and find'. With only one exception, the dogs made an excellent start, each finding the article and giving good indication. With the drugs search dogs, the method of indication I was teaching them, was to bark on finding the hidden drugs. With the explosives search dogs, they were being trained to go into the sit position on finding the hidden explosives. The one dog that was not showing the right aptitude for searching, I decided to give it a couple of days and if it did not improve, I would have to change it.

On the Sunday, we made another early start, with tracking on open ground near to the Centre.

Again we had a successful session with all the dogs performing simple one leg tracks. All the search dogs performed some good finds, giving good indications. Obviously, at the time, I was setting the dogs very simple searches in order to encourage them to search and to give the handlers plenty of opportunity to recognise the indications given by the dogs. One has to be very careful at this stage, as over- praising the dog could have the effect of eliciting from it premature indications, in order to please the handler, and get praised. Later that morning, I tested all the guard-dogs for aggression and was well pleased with the results. When we had a break at 9am, I met the Assistant Director of Security at Karachi Airport and had a long discussion on the use of dogs at the Airport for drugs and explosives detection.

At 8pm that evening, I was collected from the hotel and taken to the home of Brian Watkins for dinner. At the house I met his wife, Libby, and their two visitors from Wales, Jane and Christopher, a solicitor and barrister from Bridgend, also Norbert and his wife Olga. Olga was English, from the Tyneside area. I thanked Norbert for the crate of beer that he had sent me.

After a really splendid meal, we had a pleasant evening of conversation. It was gone midnight when Norbert and Olga dropped me off at the hotel, and I went to bed after a very enjoyable day.

On the Monday morning we again made a 7am start, beginning with obedience. All the handlers were still making basic mistakes, which was to be expected. At least, the Instructors were noticing the mistakes, which was encouraging, and they could be seen correcting the faults which the handlers were making. After the obedience session we got down to some more practical work of tracking, searching and guard-dog training. All round, it was a good morning's work, with all the handlers and dogs making steady progress. Later in the morning, when we had finished the practical training for the day, we retired to the Lecture Room, where I gave the Instructors a talk on 'Tracking' and 'The theory of scent.' After the talk, I told them that, towards the end of the course, I would be setting them a written exam. I think at first they thought that I was having them on, as we often had our bit of fun with each other, but I assured them that I meant what I'd said. In fact, it gave them something else to aim for, not that I doubted for one moment the fact that they were taking in all that I was teaching them.

That evening, my good friend, Anwar, picked me up from the hotel and we called on a friend of his, who was the Manager of the American Bank in Islamabad. He had a lovely German Shepherd dog, of which he was a bit concerned because it had something wrong with one of its ears. He asked me if I would have a look at the dog's ear, to see if I had seen anything like it before. He told me that he had taken the dog to the vet and had been told that they did not know what was wrong with it.

I examined the dog's ear, which was badly swollen, and immediately thought that it appeared to be a case of Haematoma, probably caused by a severe blow to the dog's ear, or severe scratching of the ear by the dog. I told Anwar's friend to take the dog back to the vet, so that he could surgically

128

open the swelling and the blood be drained away. He said that he would do this. When we saw him again about a week later, he said that he had taken the dog back to the vet who had done what I said, and that the dog's ear was now perfect. Before anyone starts congratulating me on my veterinary knowledge, let me immediately say that the only reason that I thought it was Haematoma was the fact that I had seen it in two other dogs before.

Next morning, we went to a large park on the outskirts of Rawalpindi called Ayub Park. It was an ideal area for tracking and guard-dog training, as there was plenty of space to lay several tracks without interfering with each other, and the guard-dogs had plenty of room to perform long chases. In fact, we were to use this area many times in the weeks to come. By now the search dogs and handlers understood what was needed of them, and all the dogs were easily finding the search article and giving good indications. The one dog that I'd had doubts about its searching ability, I changed in the second week, and its replacement soon caught up with the other dogs.

By now, I was able to dispense with the search article, which I had provided to the dog handlers at the start of the course, and use the actual substance, narcotics or explosives for all of the searches. I found that this caused no problems; all the dogs continued to find the substance without too much bother. Obviously, I was still keeping the searches rather basic, in order to further increase the confidence of the handlers and dogs.

I had a long discussion with the Instructors before finishing that day on all that we had done up to now, and stressed to them the danger that, because things had been going so well, there was always the possibility of trying to rush things to try and get ahead of the standard that we were now at.

I emphasised the fact that there was no short cut to dog training. Trying to do things beyond the dog's present standard could undo hours of hard work. I then told the Instructors that, from now on, they were each to take charge of the training of their respective groups, and that I would be there to give guidance and advice and to correct any faults in the training.

On the Wednesday morning, it was raining very heavily when I arrived at the Dog Centre, so I decided that we would begin in the Lecture Room until the rain eased off. I gave the Instructors a talk on the 13-week Police Dog Handlers Course and the Use of Police Dogs in British Police Forces.

By 10am the rain had eased off and we carried out drugs and explosives search training, using the dog handlers living quarters. It was the first time that we had introduced the dogs to an environment where people were living, sleeping and eating. It was something completely new to the dogs, but they took it in their stride and all, without exception, searched well and gave good indications. All the handlers by now where beginning to develop a system and were able to direct their dogs to different locations during the search without disturbing the dogs' concentration, and I found this encouraging. Because all the dogs were now carrying out searches without any problems, I felt that I could begin to set up more difficult hides for them all. Up to now, I'd been concealing the drugs and explosives at ground level, or a little above, but with the standard they were now at, the hides from now on would be in far more inaccessible places, e.g., inside the engine compartment of vehicles, on high shelves, down manholes, etc.

At about 11am the rain had stopped, so we all left in a large Army truck for some open ground between Rawalpindi and Islamabad for some tracking training. When we arrived at the site it began to rain again very heavily, but I decided that now that we were there we would carry on with the training.

We laid some tracks on bare hard-packed earth, which again was something new to the dogs, but they all performed two very good tracks of one leg in spite of the heavy rain. Of course, the tracks were only ten minutes old and the humidity greatly assisted the dogs. It brought back memories for me of when, with my police dog Abi, in 1966, we won the Wales and South West England Police Dog Championships, when we had full marks in the Two Hour Track, which we performed in torrential rain. A very hot sun and a drying wind cause far worse conditions than rain. After the two tracks, we were all absolutely soaked to the skin, so we returned to the Dog Centre to dry off.

The tracking we performed that day at least had the effect of proving to the handlers that rain did not have so much an adverse effect on tracking as some of them thought. Of course, in a country like Pakistan where the humidity is high, this initiates bacterial activity, which greatly increases the scent of the track, hence, increasing the dogs' chances of success.

That evening, I held a dog training session for my civilian class in a park near the Holiday Inn. During the remainder of my stay in Pakistan the training classes became very popular and grew in size. Most of the dog owners were from the Embassies and of course, some Pakistanis. They were of many nationalities, American, Dutch, German, Mexican, Norwegian, Australian etc. and were a very enthusiastic lot. I made many friends at the training sessions, which did much to alleviate my homesickness when I wasn't working at the Army Dog Centre.

Obviously, word was getting about, and the class was getting bigger every time. Later, I went home with Anwar. Eve and her husband called and, of course, we spent a couple of hours talking 'dogs'. It was what they wanted and I was only too happy to oblige.

Next day, I was over the moon with the standard of all the dogs. All the tracking dogs performed tracks of three legs, 20 minutes old, negotiating all the turns with no problem. The guard-dogs were coming on to the arm with good determined bites and instantly leaving on command. The search dogs were all giving positive indications on finding, even though I had made the hides much more difficult and out of reach of the dogs. All in all, it was a good day's work and put everyone concerned in a good mood. Back at the Dog Centre, I had a long discussion on narcotics and explosives search dogs with the Assistant Director of Security at Karachi Airport. It was decided that we would visit Islamabad Airport, with all the search dogs, for training in the near future. Before leaving the Dog Centre that day, I had a long talk with all the Instructors on the danger of the dog handlers getting too sure of themselves and trying to

131

advance too quickly, by attempting to make the dogs do something that was beyond their present stage of training. I gave specific orders that none of the dog handlers were to carry out any training other than obedience without the Instructors being present.

As I was leaving the Dog Centre I was handed a letter from Brigadier Zaidi, inviting me to be guest speaker at the annual Remount, Veterinary and Farms Corps Conference to be held at the Remount Depot, Mona, on 26th October 1985. Needless to say, I was honoured and delighted to accept the invitation.

At about 10pm that night, I put through a telephone call to Sybil and Lydia. It was good to hear their voices and it did much to lessen my feeling of homesickness.

The next two days were my rest days. My friends, Anwar Husain and Anwar Shah, were going to Lahore on business on the Saturday and had asked me if I wished to go with them. I obviously jumped at the chance of seeing this fascinating city.

On the Saturday morning I was picked up from the hotel at 5am and we left on our journey to Lahore, a distance of about 280 kilometres, with Anwar Shah driving. The journey down and back, and the sights that I saw on that day, is something that I will never forget. The roads were nothing like in this country. On the very best sections there was only a comparatively narrow strip of metal road, with hard- packed earth on either side. Brightly-decorated buses and lorries constantly ply up and down the roads, taking people and goods from town to town in a never ending round of movement and commerce. Many of the buses, all brightly coloured, had as many people on the roofs and clinging to the sides, as there was inside the bus. They say that the most ornate vehicles get the most passengers.

All along the journey there were dozens of wayside rest-houses and eating stalls, where, at any time of the day or night, travellers can get a refreshing drink or food. On the way to Lahore, we stopped off at Gujranwala, and I was taken to see the little workshops, with hard-packed earthen floors, where, using the most basic tools, products where being made of

132

outstanding quality. In one little workshop, they were making centrifugal water pumps, the like of which I have never seen better, without a modern tool in sight. It was a credit to them.

As we approached the city of Lahore, we passed the tall monument of Minar-e-Pakistan, built to symbolize the spirit of Pakistan Resolution of 1940. Right at the end of my visit to Pakistan, this monument was going to mean something more to me.

We arrived in the very busy and crowded city of Lahore about mid-day. I was taken to see Lahore Fort and the huge Badshahi Mosque, two awe-inspiring buildings. The Shish Mahal (Palace of Mirrors), a magnificent edifice inside Lahore Fort, has to be seen to be believed. Also the Diwan-e-Aam (Hall of Public Audience) built by Shah Jehan in Lahore Fort in 1631. It is where the common people used to petition the Emperor and request the settlement of disputes. The architecture of the building and the brightly coloured mosaics on the inner walls were breath- taking.

I was also taken to Lahore's bustling Anarkali Bazar, teeming with shoppers in search of bargains.

Lahore is regarded as the cultural, architectural and artistic centre of Pakistan. It is a city so steeped in historical distinction that one could spend a lifetime studying it and still not know half of its history. It is Pakistan's second largest city, with a population of over 2.5 million. I consider myself very privileged in having had the opportunity to visit this ancient and beautiful city. Our return journey to Islamabad was during the hours of darkness and was quite frightening, due to the standard of driving. Many vehicles were being driven in the pitch dark without any lights on, and you'd often find one coming towards you on your side of the road.

Still, when I got back to the hotel late that night, I knew that I'd experienced a day that would live in my memory for ever.

After two very pleasant days off, I was quite ready to get back to work at the Dog Centre on the Sunday morning. As it was, the day turned out to be a big disappointment. A new area that I was taken to proved to be completely unsuitable for

133

tracking training for the stage that the dogs had reached. It was all very rough stoney ground, with no vegetation, and large boulders strewn all over the place.

I did not attempt to lay any tracks, as failure for the dogs at this stage would have completely shattered the handlers' confidence. It would have been an example of trying to run before we could walk. I explained the situation to everyone and then decided that we would use the area for guard-dog training as we were there, and I did not want to waste time.

Later in the morning we went to a large store in an Army camp in Rawalpindi for search dog training and that was equally disappointing as it was full of foodstuffs and bags of powdered milk. The interior of the building was very dusty, not ideal conditions for search dog training.

After a couple of searches, I could see that the dogs were struggling, so I set up some hides outside so that the dogs could finish the session on a happy note. Outside was a completely different story; all the dogs completed their searches with good indications. When I got back to the hotel at the end of the day's training, I had a telephone call from Norbert and Olga, inviting me to their home for a meal, which made a pleasant end to an otherwise disappointing day.

The next day we went to a large Sports Centre in Islamabad for tracking training. We weren't using the actual arena, but there was lots of ground adjacent which was used for parking. It proved to be a good venue with plenty of room to lay several tracks, which was now needed, as the dogs were now performing tracks of 4 and 5 legs at 20 minutes to half an hour old. The ground at the sports centre was not that easy for tracking, but the results that day showed how much the dogs were improving. They were all, by now, very characteristic, with the head down posture, sniffing the ground for evidence. The basic orientation of the tracking dog is to the footsteps. It could now be said that the successful method of training dogs to track, which I had spoken about on my first visit to the Dog Centre the previous year, was now becoming evident. Later that morning we went to the Army Mounted Centre in

Rawalpindi for search dog training. I wanted to use as many different kinds of locations as possible, so as the dogs and handlers did not get into the habit of using stereotype buildings. The wider variety of locations used, the more confident the dogs become in searching. At the Mounted Centre, although completely new to the dogs, and with the smell and noise of horses, they all carried out excellent searches with good indications. All the training by the dog handlers up to now had been under strict supervision, apart from obedience training. Fortunately, the search dog handlers could not carry out any search training without the Instructors or myself being present, because they did not have any narcotics or explosive materials to use. Experienced supervision during initial training is essential, to prevent any faults going unnoticed, and therefore developing into bad habits.

When I got back to the Holiday Inn at lunch time that day, I had an invitation to attend a lunch at the hotel, which was being held in honour of Mr David Mellor, MP, Parliamentary Under Secretary of State in the Home Office, U K. I met Mr Mellor and the Prime Minister of Pakistan, Mr Mohammed Khan Junejo. There were many other VIPs present, including members of the Pakistan Narcotics Control Board. I had a long discussion with them on the use of drugs search dogs.

That evening, I held another dog training session for the civilian class at the local park. The size of the class was growing all the time, and I remember hoping that they would continue with the training after I'd left Pakistan, because the enthusiasm shown by them at the time meant that it could easily develop into a permanent Dog Training Club. It would be good for all the dog owners in the area.

During the next few days we used the Army Engineers Depot for search dog training. Again, it was a completely different environment to what the dogs had worked in before. Once again, it posed no difficulty for the dogs and they all performed excellent finds.

It was now becoming increasingly obvious to everyone that the methods of training we were adopting were highly successful, and this was raising the confidence and enthusiasm of all the handlers as well as the Instructors. It may sound ridiculous, but without anyone's knowledge, I was trying to slow things down a little, as I did not want them to 'run away with themselves'. It was all right when I was there to control matters, but if the dogs progressed too quickly, the handlers would not pick up the necessary experience to handle any problems which might occur later on.

It is always possible for a dog to 'break down', due to the inexperience of the handler in certain situations. It is then that the matter can only be put right by someone with enough knowledge of dog training to recognise what caused the problem and how to rectify it.

Next day we again went to Ayub Park for tracking and guard-dog training. This was one of the best venues we had used, because the size of the area and the ground surface provided perfect tracking conditions. Again all the tracks performed by the dogs were excellent. We then concentrated on the guard-dog group. By now all the dogs were performing 'chase and attack' off the leash, and coming in with strong and aggressive bites on the arm. I acted as 'criminal' each time, because at this stage, I did not want anything to happen which might put the dogs off attacking. As the dogs' confidence was increasing, so was the intensity of the dogs' bite on my arm. By the time that all the dogs had had two or three runs each, my arm under the leather protective sleeve was quite numb.

After this we went to the Engineers' Depot for search dog training. All the dogs again carried out their finds without any difficulty, despite the occasional fault by the handlers. I was now making the hides much more difficult and using much smaller quantities of drugs and explosive substance.

Next day was the thirteenth day since we had started the training course, and I have two reasons for making mention of this. Firstly, because on that day all the dogs performed tracks of five and six legs, all half an hour old with cross tracks included. I included the cross tracks just as an experiment and to prove a point that I had made some time before, regarding how dogs could be trained to track in a relatively short time by using the correct methods. I emphasized to the Instructors that, despite the tremendous success on that day by the dogs, it was a 'one off' for the time being, and that we were not going to rush things, but to make steady progress in the manner that I had always stated. The second reason for noting this particular day was because of the success also by the search dogs, and what happened at the end of the training session.

That day we carried out our search training in a very large hangar-type building, in which was stored mechanical and engineering equipment. Again as a 'one-off' experiment, I set up some very difficult hides, firstly for the drugs dogs and then for the explosives dogs. Every one of the dogs, without exception, performed a perfect search and find and gave excellent indications.

This put everyone in really high spirits.

Just as we were preparing to leave the venue, two vans arrived with two fully-trained drugs dogs and their handlers, who had been trained in Germany. I immediately thought that this would be an ideal opportunity to show the handlers and Instructors on the course what can be achieved when their dogs are fully trained, so I asked the two handlers via Major Chugtai who was with us, if they where prepared to demonstrate to the course how fully trained dogs worked, and they agreed. I then went in to parts of the building that we hadn't used, and set up some very easy hides of drugs substance, because I wanted the dogs to be successful for the benefit of the handlers and Instructors watching.

The first dog searched in a very lethargic manner and eventually found one of the hides, but gave a poor indication, which I'm sure the handler didn't see. The second dog did not find any of the hides at all and was very poorly handled. All this was witnessed by Major Chugtai, the Officer in Charge of the Dog Centre, by the Instructors and all the handlers.

My reason for the demonstration had back-fired, as my intention had been for the handlers and Instructors to see dogs working at a standard which they were aiming for. As it was, the dogs on the course, after only 13 days training, were far better than the fully trained dogs. I felt very embarrassed for the two handlers and was sorry that I had involved them.

I immediately suspected that the reason for the poor performance by the two trained dogs, was lack of proper continuation training and I later took advantage of pointing this out to the Instructors.

It matters not how good the initial training of the dog is, if this is not followed up by regular continuation training, in order to maintain the standard required. Experience has taught that complacency is the greatest enemy of the operational search dog handler. Even with careful selection of handlers, it is very easy for a handler to become over-confident or satisfied with his own and his dog's standard of ability. Each dog and handler must, as a minimum, have one annual refresher course. Ideally, each dog and handler should attend a refresher course every six months, and continuation training under supervision, carried out on a regular basis in between.

On the Thursday morning, Brigadier Zaidi, the Director of the Remount, Veterinary and Farms Corps and Colonel Quaiser, Deputy Director, accompanied us to Ayub Park to watch the tracking and guard-dogs training. All of the dogs performed excellent tracks of three legs, half an hour old, and the guard-dogs all carried out their chase and attack exercises without any problems. Brigadier Zaidi said that he was very impressed with the standard of all the dogs and he thanked me for coming to Pakistan and imparting my knowledge to the Instructors. He said that they were going to adopt my methods of training on all their future courses.

On the Friday, my day off, Anwar and Najma took me to Wah to visit their friends, Farouk and his family. On the way to Wah we visited Taxila Museum. Anwar told the Curator at the museum that I was a visitor from the UK and, for the next hour, a guide took me around the museum and explained many of things on view, and of the 2,000 year old ruins of the ancient city nearby, which was once a centre of learning and of Buddhist culture. It was a fascinating narration, and very informative.

On arrival at Farouk's home, and after a lovely lunch specially prepared by Farouk's wife for my liking, we all went to Wah Gardens. Much of the ancient bathing pools and walkways were now in ruins, but it was still a very beautiful place and very peaceful. On looking around, it was easy to imagine its splendour many, many years before.

Late in the afternoon we made out way back to Islamabad, because at 5.30pm we had a dog training session for our civilian class, which once again was very well attended. After the dog training class, Eve and Marie Jo took me back to their home for a meal before taking me back to the hotel. Before leaving their home, I said good-bye to Eve's husband Anwar, as he was going back to his farm in Karachi.

Sunday,20th October, was a day that I could well have done without. Arriving back at the hotel from the Army Dog Centre at about 12.20pm, I decided to go down to the shops for a walk and do a bit of shopping, after which I spent a little time in the hotel swimming pool.

At about 4pm, I was lying on my bed reading, when the telephone rang. It was the hotel under-manager. He politely asked me if I could vacate my room in the next hour, as he had other people waiting for the room. I obviously thought that he had made some mistake or that there had been a misunderstanding with the booking, and told him that I would come down to see him. At reception, the under-manager was very apologetic, but explained that the British Embassy had only booked the room until 10th October, and that I'd been staying there since on a day-to-day basis. He went on to explain that all the rooms were fully booked, and that he had no other room to give me.

I'd had no warning of this and was quite shocked. The under-manager was quite concerned but I told him that it was not his fault. I then telephoned the British Embassy and told them of the situation. I also telephoned my friend, Anwar, and he immediately came to the hotel. I packed all my things and brought my baggage down to reception. After about half an hour, the

Second Secretary (Aid) and the TCO (Admin) from the British Embassy arrived at the hotel. The Second Secretary said that he would sort the matter out and went to the hotel desk. I had already been told by the under-manager that there were no rooms available and I had told the Second Secretary this. He came back from the hotel desk and said that there was nothing that the hotel could do to help me, which I already knew. The Second Secretary seemed unsure as to what to do, though he said that he would try to book me into another hotel. I politely but firmly told him that I would do this myself.

The only other decent hotel was the Islamabad Hotel, which was a large complex like the Holiday Inn. Anwar took me to this hotel, but they had no vacancies for at least a week. This left me with no alternative but to book into a very poor class hotel on the edge of the city. I telephoned the Army Dog Centre to let them know my new address for my driver to be able to pick me up in the morning. My room was quite shabby, and the bed was hard and uncomfortable. There was no toilet paper in the bathroom, and I had to shave and shower in near-cold water the whole time that I was there. There were many Afghans staying at the hotel, and every time I left, or came into, the hotel they would be standing in groups, looking at me and muttering to themselves. It could be quite scary, but it didn't bother me.

I didn't sleep at all the first night, and was up at 4.00am writing my notes. Before being picked up by my driver at 6.20am, I had to shave in water that was almost ice cold. The bonus was, getting away from the hotel for as long as possible.

We had another excellent day with the dogs that day, using opium with the drugs search dogs for the first time. They were all finding and giving good indications, and I can honestly say that this progress continued for the rest of the time that I was in Pakistan.

Another good friend that I made through the civilian dog training class, was an elderly lady called Ann Ransome. Ann had worked for the British Embassy for many years and, when she retired, had decided to settle in Pakistan, because that was where most of her friends now lived.

Ann lived in a nice bungalow which she had designed herself. She attended the dog training classes with her little dog, which, if I remember rightly, was a spaniel. Ann was a lovely lady.

After I'd been at this change of hotel for a couple of days, it might have been a coincidence, but I had terrible stomach pains and diarrhoea, and generally feeling quite unwell. I was hardly sleeping at all any night. Anwar kept taking me to his home, or out visiting most evenings, but it was the nights that I was really dreading, being unable to sleep properly. As often as they'd let me, I would take Anwar and his wife, and Eve and Marie Jo out for a meal. It was the least that I could do after all the hospitality that they had been showing me. I don't know what I would have done without them.

At the Dog Centre, I kept using as many different venues for training as I could, especially for the search dogs, to give them a wide variety of environments. We were now using Islamabad Airport and Rawalpindi Railway Station quite regularly. Both these venues were real testing grounds, but posed no problems for the dogs.

On the Wednesday evening, Ann picked me up to go to dog training. Eleven people turned up with their dogs. It was encouraging to see how much the dogs were improving, and how enthusiastic the owners were to learn new things. Laura, one of the class members, invited me to come to her home for a meal on Friday evening. I told her that I would be delighted to come.

After training class, I went home with Anwar and, on the way, we called at the Islamabad Hotel to see if there were any vacancies. We were told that there might be after the weekend. Anwar also had some American friends at his home for dinner that evening and, after a lovely meal which Najma had cooked, we spent a couple of hours talking. Yes, again, mostly about dogs.

At 11pm, the Americans dropped me off at the hotel. (Note that I say, 'the hotel' and not 'my hotel', I wonder why?) Before going to bed, I asked at reception if they could book me a telephone call to the UK. It never materialised.

Each day now at the Dog Centre, I could see much improvement with the dogs and handlers.

The Instructors, obviously with their keenness and enthusiasm, had become quite competent in correcting any faults made by the handlers, and also at handling their own dogs. As well as all the hides for the search dogs more difficult, I was also introducing the tracking dogs to different types of ground surface and putting more acute turns into the tracks and adding cross tracks. On Thursday, Colonel Quaiser said that he wanted me to meet some officials from the Ministry of Defence the next week to discuss future training for the Explosives Search Dogs.

When I returned to my room in the hotel at about 12.30pm that day, I found an unused bullet standing upright on the cabinet beside the bed. It had definitely not been there when I left that morning. At the time I thought that many men at the hotel (there were no women staying there) saw me being picked up by an Army driver each morning, and the Army was not very popular with many. It did make me think, 'was there any significance in the bullet being in my room?' Still, I put the bullet in my pocket, and thought no more about it.

That afternoon I hired a taxi to take me to the British Embassy to collect my subsistence.

When I was speaking to John Ellis, the treasurer, I remembered the bullet and showed it to him.

I then left to go back to the hotel.

Before going in to the hotel, I went for a walk to the shops to start looking for presents to bring home for Sybil and the rest of my family. Finding something for Sybil and the girls was no problem, as there was plenty of jewellery about, but what was I going to get for my two sons-in-law?

When I got back to the hotel, there was a message in reception for me to telephone a Mr Goodenough at the British Embassy. I immediately telephoned, and Mr Goodenough introduced himself to me as Head of Security at the Embassy. He said that John Ellis had told him about me finding a bullet in my room and asked me if I was worried about it. He spoke of the Indian Diplomat that had been killed in England and the fact that there was some 'anti' feeling against England by Sikh extremists.

He suggested that the bullet may have been found on the floor by a cleaner, who might have thought that it was mine. I told Mr Goodenough that I had thought exactly the same myself and that I was not worried in any way. He then asked if I wished to come and stay at his home. After thanking him very much for his concern, I said that I would stay where I was.

I knew that, with a bit of luck, I'd be staying at the Islamabad Hotel in a few days. We decided that I would speak to the hotel manager about my finding the bullet, to try and clarify the matter. I told Mr Goodenough that I would call him back later.

I then spoke to the hotel manager and showed him the bullet. He said that he would check with the cleaner, and then spoke to someone on the telephone in Urdu. When he put the telephone down, he told me that the cleaner had found the bullet on the floor of my room and asked me if I wanted to move to another room. I thought to myself, 'I want to move to another hotel', but thanked him and said that I would stay where I was. I again telephoned Mr Goodenough with the result and thanked him very much for his concern in the matter.

By now, with the way that things were working out at the Dog Centre, I knew how much more time I needed to complete the training of the dogs and handlers and for the lectures to the Instructors. I contacted the British Embassy and asked them to book me a British Airways flight home for Thursday, 7th November. That gave me 12 more days to complete my assignment.

That evening, I had a taxi out to Norbert and Olga's house, where I'd been invited to a cocktail party, being held in the honour of Norbert's boss, who had arrived from Germany. When I arrived, Norbert asked me if I would keep company with another guest, who also did not know anyone present. He said that I might have heard of him, as he used to play professional football in England. He said his name was Bert Trautmann and introduced me to him. I immediately said that I knew who he was, as I shook hands with him. He was a very

143

sociable and friendly person, and said to me that I was only saying that I knew him, to be kind. I then said to him, 'You played in goal for Manchester City, and you broke your neck playing in the Cup Final.'

I have never seen a man looking more pleased. He put his arms around me and said, 'You do know who I am.' He had a very British accent, with a slight lilt of Welsh, and told me that he used to live in Anglesey. He was in Pakistan, coaching the Pakistan National Football Team. We became firm friends during the rest of his stay in Pakistan.

When I returned to the hotel late that evening, I asked if I could book a call to the UK and was again told that the line was not working.

I was 'day off' the next day and got up about 7am, although I'd been awake most of the night. I went down to the hotel restaurant, which I'd hardly used, as I was feeling a little hungry. I had a type of cornflakes with hot milk (there was no cold), an omelette, and toast and marmalade.

It was edible, just about.

After breakfast, I went down to the Islamabad Hotel and, when they told me that they would have a vacancy after Sunday, I booked a room as from the Monday. I explained that I would be away from the area for the week-end and that I would be arriving at the hotel late afternoon on the Monday. I then went back to the hotel where I was staying, as I had a heavy cold and was feeling quite miserable. I thought that I was in for a lonely day, as Anwar was also ill at home. I had a dog training class at 5pm, but that was a long way off and I thought that the day would drag.

I hadn't been back in my room more than 10 minutes, when the telephone rang, and I was told that I had a visitor in reception. I went down and there was Eve. She said that she knew that Anwar was ill, so she thought, as it was my day off, she would take me out for some sight-seeing. What a pal! Although she's French, she is so British in her ways. She is a teacher in the International School in Islamabad.

She took me first to Rawal Lake, which is one of the local

144

beauty spots, and I was able to take some lovely photographs, although I had been there before on my first visit to Pakistan. She then took me to a Riding School, and then to see a typical Pakistani village. At about 2.15pm she dropped me off at the hotel, because she had some work to do, before our dog training class.

I stayed in my room until Ann Ransome picked me up at about 4.30pm to go to the park, for our dog training session. After dog training, I went home with Laura and her husband, Derek. Laura is Mexican, and Derek is Australian. Eve also came, as did Carol and Bob, who are Americans and had two Pointer dogs. Also present were two other men who worked with Derek, one a New Zealander and another Australian. We had a lovely meal with Laura and Derek and then spent the evening talking 'dogs'.

Eve and I left about 10pm and, before taking me back to the hotel, she took me to the Telephone Exchange, so that I could telephone Sybil. Eve knew that I was worried because I had been unable to telephone her for so long. At the Telephone Exchange, one of the operators tried to get through for about 15 minutes. I could see that Eve was watching him and was getting hot under the collar. She leaned over the counter and said, 'Give it here', taking the handset out of the operator's hand. After about half a minute's dialling, she handed me the set, and I was talking to Sybil. It was so good to hear her voice, and I was quite relieved.

We also called at the Holiday Inn, and there were two letters there for me. One from my daughter, Marianne, and the other from my daughter, Jeannette. When Eve dropped me off at the hotel, she said for me to make sure that I put the chain on my door, as there were a lot of Afghans staying at the hotel. I don't want to sound melodramatic, but, before retiring for the night, I took out my lock-knife, opened it , and put it on the cabinet beside my bed. I don't know what I was going to do with it if someone did come in.

On the Saturday morning, I was quite elated getting up, as I had just spent my last night at the hotel. After a wash and shave

145

in cold water, I didn't bother going down for breakfast, but was only too happy to finish my packing. That morning we were leaving for Mona to attend the annual Remount, Veterinary and Farms Corps, Conference. When I was picked up by my driver, after paying my hotel bill, I took all my baggage with me, as I did not want to return to the hotel again before checking in to the Islamabad Hotel on the Monday, when we returned from Mona.

After tea and biscuits at the Dog Centre, we left to travel down to Mona, a journey of about five hours. I travelled down in the staff car, accompanied by Major Mqbool, one of the Instructors on my course.

On the way down, we called at the town of Gujrat, well know for its furniture-making, and arrived at the Remount Depot, Mona, at about 4.30pm. Over the main gates leading in to the Depot, it read in big metal letters 'The Home of Horses', and believe me, there could not be a truer statement. It is the breeding and training centre for all the horses in the Pakistan Army, comprising of 10,000 acres, and is completely self-sufficient, growing all its own fodder.

At the Depot they had two cross- country courses, several dressage areas, schooling areas, jumping arenas and two polo grounds.

When we arrived at the Depot, they were waiting for me and, after tea and biscuits, I was taken to my room in the Officers Mess. It was a lovely bedroom with a dressing room and bathroom.

After a wash and tidy-up, I took a walk around the main building. In the front hall-way, there were large framed photographs of all the former Directors of the Remount, Veterinary and Farms Corps. The Depot itself, was founded by Colonel Templar in 1902.

Later, I was introduced to everyone present. The Conference itself was for officers of the Regiment only. I met up again with Colonel Shafique, who was the Deputy Director at the Army Dog Centre during my first visit. It was good to see him again, and we had a long conversation about that visit. In the evening we had a buffet supper in a large marquee on the lawn in front of the Officers Mess, after which we were entertained by a PAF Band and local folk dancers. I retired to bed at 10pm and slept like a log.

On the Sunday morning I was up at 6am and went for a walk in the grounds, and to take some photographs. As I was walking through the trees, a beautifully-coloured parrot flew past me, and my immediate thought was that it must have escaped from somewhere. It was only when about a dozen others flew past, that I realised that they were wild.

After breakfast, we went to watch riders training for a three-day event, and then to see a vaulting display by 12 riders and horses. It was as good as anything one would see in a first class circus.

It was the second day of the conference and, as guest speaker, I was on at 10.45am. My talk on 'The Training and Deployment of Service Dogs' was extremely well received and I had a standing ovation. Many came up to me afterwards and said that they had never heard a more practical, informative and frank talk. Captain Raza, one of the Instructors on the course, said how refreshing it was, after listening to dry subjects like feeding cattle and nutrition. He also said, 'When you were speaking, there was no danger of anyone going to sleep.'

After my talk, I stayed on to listen to some of the other speakers, who were all military personnel. At 1.30pm we had lunch, and I said good-bye to some of the other speakers who were leaving. Later, Major Maqbool was assigned to take me on a conducted tour of the whole Depot in a 'two in hand', which is an open coach drawn by two horses, with a driver and attendant. It was a most fascinating tour, I have never seen so many horses in my life, and really, I did not see half of what they had at the Depot.

There were literally dozens and dozens of horses everywhere. I saw a batch of about 50 breeding mares, which had recently been shipped in from Vienna and Argentina, and countless numbers of mules, which are bred for carrying supplies to the soldiers based in the mountains in Kashmir. There were corals

147

all over the place, filled with horses, many of them young and as yet untrained. From a horse lover's point of view, I have never seen such an impressive sight in my life.

Early that evening, after having a shower, I sat in the lounge with the senior officers, which included Brigadier Zaidi and Colonel Shafique. Dinner was then served in the large Arab-style tent on the front lawn, after which I had an early night, probably catching up on the sleep which I had lost in my last hotel.

Next morning, before breakfast, I again sat in the lounge with the senior officers, who were still saying how much they had enjoyed my talk the day before. After breakfast and saying all my good-byes, I left in a staff car with Major Kalid Chugtai and Major Malik Zia.

On the journey back to Rawalpindi, we called at the military farm in Jhelum, and then at the Jhelum Military Veterinary Hospital, where we had lunch with Captain Muhammad Amir.

We arrived back in Rawalpindi about mid-afternoon and, after collecting my baggage from the Army Dog Centre, I checked into the Islamabad Hotel. After my previous hotel, I felt as if I was in Heaven.

Early evening I was picked up by Ann to go to our dog training class at a new venue, the Exhibition Ground. It was a bit dusty, but gave us more room, as the class was continually getting bigger. After dog training I went home with Anwar for the evening. I got back to my room in the Islamabad Hotel by 9.30pm and soon fell asleep, as I was dead tired after a memorable weekend.

By now, at the Dog Centre, all the dogs were successfully performing half hour old tracks of several legs. All the handlers had confidence in their dogs' ability and were no longer trying to think for the dog: a good sign that they were leaving the novice stage. The guard dogs in the 'chase and attack' exercise were all coming strongly on to the arm and, almost without exception, leaving with one word of command. Over the last couple of weeks, after all of the dogs had developed a good firm bite, I had concentrated on the dogs being a little less

148

aggressive, and putting more emphasis on control. With the search dogs, I was now able to conceal the explosives and narcotics substance at the bottom of a hold-all type bag, filled with clothes, and conceal the bag way out of reach of the dogs. Without exception, they were finding and giving good indications each time. It was now obvious to everyone concerned, the handlers, the Instructors and all the staff at the Dog Centre, that the methods of training that we had used over the past weeks had been highly successful. There's an old saying, 'the proof of the pudding is in the eating' and I didn't think that anyone could argue with the results we had achieved.

On Wednesday 30th October, I had a meeting with several officials from the Ministry of Defence, and we discussed in detail the future training and deployment of explosives search dogs in the Pakistan Army.

During my time in Pakistan, I had been to some wonderful places, and seen many memorable sights, but little did I know that it was not yet over. On Friday 1st November, my day off, Colonel Quaiser and his army driver picked me up from the hotel at 8.30am, and we drove up to Peshawar, a journey of about three hours. After some sight-seeing on the way, we arrived at the Military Veterinary Hospital, Peshawar, just after 12noon, and were met by the Officer in Charge, Lt. Colonel Manzoor Ahmad, Major Gulzar Hussain and Captain Usman Nasir. They were expecting me and gave me a wonderful welcome. I had met Lt. Colonel Ahmad at the annual conference in Mona, and he said that my visit was their way of thanking me for the talk that I had given at the conference.

After a light meal, Major Hussain took Colonel Quaiser and me up into the hills towards the Khyber Pass, and what I saw in the next couple of hours was something one would only expect to see in the films.

On a plateau, high up in the hills, I was to see a spectacle that one could only describe as unbelievable. On a large area of rough ground, which was not marked out as a pitch, there were two teams of about 20 mounted tribesmen from Pakistan, Afghanistan and Kashmir. They were a really fierce looking crowd, and they all carried leather bull whips. They were to take part in what they call Buzz Kashy (calf dragging). At one end of the area, there was a pole stuck in the ground, and, at the other end of the area, there was a circle painted on the ground. In the middle of the arena there was the carcass of a calf, weighing about 120lbs. The object of the contest (or war) was that, at the start, anyone from either team would try to pick up the carcass without dismounting, and then, carrying the carcass with one hand whilst controlling the horse with the other hand, gallop to the end of the area where the pole was, go around the pole, and then gallop at full speed to the other end where the circle was, and drop the carcass in the circle.

Now, I reckon, considering the weight of the carcass, that would be quite a feat in itself, but, although the team mates of the man carrying the carcass were trying to protect him as he galloped along, members of the opposing team could do anything, and I mean anything, to prevent him from picking up the carcass, or to make him drop it as he was carrying it. They were slashing at him and his horse with their bull whips as they all galloped along. There were several riders with open wounds on their faces dripping with blood from slashes made by the bull whips. The horses were also being slashed, and you could see the weals on the horses bodies, and some with open wounds. There appeared to be no rules whatsoever and spectators were being knocked over and trampled by the horses as they galloped past. I took many photographs, but often had to dive out of the way to prevent being trampled to death.

Unfortunately, the still photographs I took, do not show the true story; I only wished that I'd had a camcorder with me. I was told that, up in that area, near the Khyber Pass, it was a regular event. After leaving the 'war zone', we went to the home of Lt Colonel Ahmad, where we had a lovely meal.

All of the officers were ardent polo-players and, after lunch, we all went to the Peshawar Polo Ground, together with the families, to watch two polo games. Lt. Colonel Ahmad was playing in one of the teams, and Captain Nasir was one of the umpires. It was a lovely afternoon's sport, especially after what

150

I had seen a short time before. At half time, Colonel Quaiser took me into Peshawar itself, to see the Qissa Khawani Bazaar, Peshawar's famous 'Street of Story Tellers'.

When we returned to the polo ground, the games were just coming to an end, and we all went to the home of one of the civilian polo players, Raza Kuli Khan, for tea. At 6.30pm we left Peshawar to return to Islamabad to end another most spectacular day.

At the Dog Centre, I had now introduced heroin, and other new types of explosives to the search dog teams, and once again it proved to be no problem; they were all finding and indicating well. We were now regularly visiting Rawalpindi Railway Station for our searching exercises, using the large goods-sheds, full of all types of freight. It was really quite a difficult venue for the dogs at this stage of the training, but I knew that so long as I kept a close watch on the proceedings, no harm could be done. It also gave the handlers and dogs experience in having to work in an environment where there were many people moving about in the near vicinity, so that the dogs could get used to ignoring people and get on with the searching. All the dogs were finding the substance and giving good indications.

My only concern now was, whether or not this training would be maintained after I had left Pakistan. As any experienced dog trainer knows, continuation and refresher training are of utmost importance. A handler cannot assume that once a dog has learned a particular exercise, it has learned it for all time. The learning process must be reinforced throughout the dog's working life, or the efficiency of the dog will lapse.

On my next dog training session with the civilian class in Islamabad on Saturday 2nd November, we had it on video. I gave an exhibition of obedience using Shane, Eve's dog. I emphasised oral and visual commands, positioning of oneself and the dog and basic faults.

It was something that they could refer to in future training sessions. After training class, I went with Eve and Marie Jo to

151

Ann Ramsome's home for dinner. Ann had cooked roast beef and Yorkshire Pudding especially for me; it was delicious.

On the Monday morning, I gave the Instructors the written examination which I had prepared. The results from them all were excellent, which, apart from anything else, I took as a compliment to myself, if only for the fact that it showed they had paid close attention to all that I had said during the training, and at my lectures.

That evening, Major Chugtai and all the Instructors took me out for a farewell dinner at the Shelimar Hotel in Rawalpini. It was a very pleasant evening, as we had all become very close friends during the time that I had been in Pakistan. I often think of them, and how their careers have progressed in the Army.

On the Tuesday morning I had a meeting with Mr Pervez Rehman of the Pakistan Narcotics Control Board re the future training of a dedicated unit of narcotic search dogs and handlers. In the afternoon, at the Exhibition Ground, I took my last session of the civilian dog training class. At the end everyone thanked me for the time I had spent training them over the past weeks, and they presented me with a lovely hard-covered book 'Journey through Pakistan'. They had all signed the inside cover of the book. I thanked them all for the lovely gift and said how much I had enjoyed the time I had spent with them. I told them that their enthusiasm and desire to learn had given me much pleasure.

After the class, I went home with Eve and Marie Jo for a nice meal of roast chicken, cauliflower and roast potatoes. That evening, they took me to see the play 'Two and Two make Six', at the International School. It was played by the local amateur dramatic group. When they dropped me off at the hotel, I said my good-byes to them both and thanked them for the most generous hospitality they had shown me during the whole of my stay in Pakistan. They were really good friends. I had already said my good-byes to Norbert and Olga, and to all the friends that I had made at the Australian Embassy.

Wednesday, 6th November, my last working day in Pakistan, was an extremely busy and emotional day. I was picked up by my driver at 7am. When we arrived at the Dog Centre, I was asked if I would attend another meeting with the Ministry of Defence Officials at 12 noon. I had first a general discussion with all the Instructors on all that we had covered during my visit then answered any last minute questions they had. At 10am, everyone at the Dog Centre was asked to convene at the main Lecture Room. Brigadier Zaidi, Colonel Quaiser, Major Chugtai, the Instructors and all the dog handlers were present. Major Chugai gave an opening talk, and thanked me on behalf of all the Instructors and the dog handlers for all that I had done during my stay, and for the very friendly manner in which I had carried out all my instruction to them. He said that my training methods had proved beyond doubt to be highly successful, and had improved the whole structure of the Dog Centre. Brigadier Zaidi then thanked me for the instruction and advice I had given, and said that in all his meetings with me, he had always been most impressed by my attitude of enthusiasm, competence and frankness. He went on to say that many of my training methods had already been put into operation, and many more changes would be made in the future. He then presented me with a plaque of the Remount, Veterinary and Farms Corps on behalf of the Army Dog Centre.

The Instructors then presented me with a large silver salver, embossed with Minar-e-Pakistan, the monument which I had actually seen on my visit to Lahore. They also gave me a gift for my wife. I then thanked Brigadier Zaidi, and everyone else present, for their gifts, their very kind remarks and for the exceptional hospitality they had shown me during the whole of my stay. I went on to say how easy my job had been made by the enthusiasm of everyone concerned, and by the way in which everyone had so willingly accepted my advice and instruction at all times. I said that their attitude towards the training augured well for the future of the Army Dog Centre. I then gave them a plaque of the Staffordshire Police for the Army Dog Centre.

At 12 noon, I was taken to the Ministry of Defence Offices in Rawalpindi for a further meeting with the Joint Secretary, Mr Mohammad Rashid, and other officials re the future training of explosives search dogs. When I returned to the Dog Centre, I shook hands with all the dog handlers, said my good-byes, and wished then continued success with their dogs.

Before leaving the Dog Centre, all the Instructors said that they would be at the Airport in the morning to see me off.

I had completed my assignment in Pakistan to the full satisfaction of the people concerned and I was more than happy with the way that the Army authorities had treated me and accepted me throughout the whole of my stay. It was obvious from their attitude that they were very satisfied with the results of the training programme and the standard achieved by the dogs and handlers in all exercises. When I left the Dog Centre for the last time, I must admit it was with a touch of sadness. Although I was overjoyed at the thought of going home the next day, I felt somehow, that I was leaving something behind. Over the past weeks, I had formed a strong bond of friendship with the six Instructors and the staff at the Army Dog Centre, and I knew that I was going to remember the good times that we shared for a long time to come.

Later in the afternoon Anwar picked me up from the hotel, and I spent the rest of the day with him and Najma at their home. Before he took me back to the hotel that evening, I thanked them both for being such wonderful friends and for the exceptional hospitality they had shown me, ever since I first met them. I can honestly say that if it had not been for the likes of them and some of the other friends that I had made, my off-duty time would have been very lonely. When Anwar took me back to the hotel for the last time, we didn't talk much on the journey, I think that the parting was effecting us both. When he dropped me off, he said that he would be at the Airport in the morning to say farewell.

I slept very little that last night, I think it was a mixture of leaving Pakistan and the excitement of going home. I had really enjoyed my stay in Pakistan and had made many good friends, but I had missed Sybil and the family very much and I was dying to see them.

Next morning I was up and dressed at 4.30am, although my driver wasn't picking me up until 5.45am. As it was, he was there at 5.30am and we were at the airport at 6am. Customs officers were checking all the baggage for drugs, but they didn't look at mine. They were probably fed up with seeing me at the airport. Just after I got to the airport, Anwar arrived and we said our emotional good-byes. He had been such a good friend.

Major Chugtai and all the Instructors were there in their best uniforms and, as they hugged me as they said their good-byes, I'm sure that all the other passengers were wondering what was going on. As I left the departure lounge in a Customs and Excise car to be taken out to the aircraft, a British Airways Boeing 747, they all kept waving until I was out of sight.

We took off for Abu Dhabi at 7.58am and, as we did so, I changed the time on my watch to 2.58am British Time as, after all, I was going home. As we left the airport behind us, it was a beautiful sunny morning and, apart from having a rasping cough, which I'd had for weeks, I felt really good. We landed at Abu Dhabi at 6.15am and I got off the plane and went for a walk in the terminal building. It had the most beautiful passenger lounge I had seen.

At Abu Dhabi, we picked up a new crew. There had been a steward on the top deck from Islamabad, and now we had a stewardess. There were only six passengers on the top deck, so we had good service as we took off at 7.30am. A short time later, the Captain announced that we had been refused permission to land at Dhoha for some time, as a VIP was due to take off from there and the airport had been closed to incoming flights. We had to circle for quite some time before we had clearance to land. As we came in on our final approach at 8.36am, I could see the red carpet still lined out on the Tarmac for the VIP.

The stewardess had just heard me coughing and said that she would make me a hot drink of lemon and honey. She asked me where I had picked up the cough, and I told her Pakistan and that I'd had it about three weeks. When she brought me the hot drink, which immediately soothed my chest, she said that she had the cough some time ago, and that, at the present time they had two crews down with it in the Middle East; they were marooned there, because they were not allowed to go anywhere near a plane when they had the cough.

We took off from Dhoha at 9.45am and, although there was plenty of room to lie down and sleep, I was too excited at going home, so I settled down to watch a film, 'Chariots of Fire.'

We landed at Heathrow at about 4.30pm, and I caught the shuttle flight up to Birmingham and landed at about 6.45pm. Sybil was at the airport waiting for me, and what a delight it was to see her. I had missed her so very much.

CHAPTER NINE
RETIRING FROM THE POLICE FORCE

I have always been very grateful that I was given the opportunity to go to Pakistan. Apart from the fact that I was able to share my knowledge and experience in dog training with others, it also gave me the chance to see ancient and spectacular places, and to meet people with a culture so different to that in this country. So many only read about such places, or see them on television. I will always consider it an honour to have met the people of Pakistan. Also, that travel is such a wonderful educator. The object of my visit was to teach others modern methods of dog training, but whilst I was there doing this, I learned much myself.

It gave me a chance to study more deeply the 'formulation' and 'properties' of scent in relation to tracking with a dog. I found that with the humidity of the climate, human scent on the track remained present, longer than it did in cooler drier climates. Although it is a fact that warm bodies in a cool environment will give off proportionately greater amount of scent than warm bodies in a hot environment, the important factor is the length of time that the scent remains on the ground, as opposed to the disturbed earth and crushed vegetation vapour.

When a person walks along the ground, there are two pieces of evidence present - firstly, the airborne rafts of human scent falling on to the ground - and, secondly, the physical disturbance of the earth and the crushing of vegetation. The combination of the two is considered the ground picture. Disturbance of the soil and crushing of any vegetation, releases moisture and chemical vapours, and these, together with rafts of human scent, produces bacterial activity. This intensifies with the presence of moisture, hence the track scent remains longer in humid conditions, than when it is very hot and dry.

Tracking has always been my favourite exercise in police dog work. I well remember when I had my first police dog, Abi, in the 1960's. I would go to Withybush Airfield in Haverfordwest, and watch her performing free tracks. That is, having the dog to follow a pre-laid track, without her wearing a tracking harness, and having a tracking line attached. I would put the dog down on the edge of the runway, give her the command to 'stay', and then walk off on the grass, using the whole of the airfield. I would make the track over a mile long, comprising of several legs with left and right turns, making sure that I would return to where I had left the dog from the opposite direction. I would place an article on the ground about 25 yards from the end of the track for her to find.

I would have made a rough sketch of the track on paper, showing exactly where and in what direction I had made the turns at the end of each leg, using fixed points, such as trees, posts and buildings as reference points. When I got back to the dog, I would wait about 20 minutes or so, and then take her to the start of the track and give her the command, 'seek'. Off she would go, nose down, and I would stay where I was, watching her working out the track.

Because it was open ground, with no objects in the way, I could keep her in sight as she negotiated the whole of the track. From my sketch, I knew roughly where and when she would make her turns and in which direction. She wouldn't put a foot (sorry, paw) wrong. When she reached the article near the end of the track, she would lie down, as I had trained her to do on finding articles on the track, and wait for me to go to her and give her praise.

Free tracking is a sure way to improve a dog's tracking ability. Of course, one would not do this before the dog has been trained to track with a tracking harness and line. When free tracking, the dog is not being hampered by, or getting any cues from the handler. When initially teaching a dog to track, the handler must know exactly where the track goes, where each turn is, and in which direction. He should carefully watch the track being laid, so that he is absolutely aware of the exact route. Obviously, you should always take into account the wind direction, so as not to cause any interference by incorrectly-placed articles, or other legs of the track. As with any other aspect of dog training, tracking is a very complex subject, and it would take a volume of books to cover all the ins and outs.

After a couple of days of settling back into the routine at Stafford, one of my first priorities was to put pen to paper, and record a full and detailed report of all that had transpired during my assignment to the Army Dog Centre, at Rawalpindi, Pakistan. This would of course be required by the Overseas Development Administration Department of the British Government.

The next 18 months in Stafford continued in the usual vein. I was away on numerous occasions, visiting other forces in connection with police dogs and police horses. There were the regular police dog trials, at which I would be judging or adjudicating in various parts of the country, and on the Police Mounted side, taking our horses to compete at the Horse of the Year Show at Wembley, the Royal Tournament at Earls Court, and various other police horse shows and duties.

Perhaps like many others, I believe that there comes a time in life, when one decides to call a halt to the 'old routine'. I don't know! Perhaps it's a sign of old age, or a feeling that a change is as good as a rest. Whatever the reason, in May 1987, I decided to retire from the police force.

I consider that I have been extremely lucky to have been given the chance to enjoy, and get so much satisfaction from, a career, which at the age of 28 years, I would have thought of as being nothing more than a wild dream. For that wild dream, I shall be forever grateful, and have memories that will continue to give me so much pleasure for the rest of my life. I believe that job satisfaction is priceless.

I set about putting in my notice of retirement, and tidying up any loose ends for whoever was going to be my successor. Sybil and I had decided that we would go back to the West Country to live, as that was where our immediate family now lived.

My last working day with the Staffordshire Police was 30th June 1987, so, as from the 1st July 1987, I was a police pensioner. It comes around sooner than one expects.

On the 12th July 1987, Sybil and I were invited as guests at the Staffordshire Police Horse Show, at the County Showground, Stafford. I had started the Police Horse Show during my time in Stafford and over the years it had developed into the second largest Police Horse Show in the country, after the Metropolitan Police Horse Show. The show attracted competitors from most of the Police Mounted Branches in the country.

I had been asked to present the prizes and trophies to the police winners in the main arena.

After completing the presentations, I was leaving the arena, when I heard the MC announce over the loudspeaker system that there was one more presentation to be made. I naturally thought that I had forgotten something, especially when I heard him say, 'Would Chief Inspector Phillips please return to the main arena.' On my re-entering the arena, the MC announced that that the members of the Staffordshire Police Mounted Branch and Police Dog Training School wished to make a presentation to me on my retirement and I was handed a large cardboard box. On opening the box, it contained a beautiful bronze figure of a mare with her foal, on a plinth. I was overwhelmed, and, on thanking them all, I said that it would always be given a place of prominence in my home. Sybil was presented with a lovely bouquet of flowers.

On the 22nd September 1987, I was invited to a meeting of the Home Office Standing Advisory Committee on Police Dogs (Sub Training Committee) at Durham, and was presented with an inscribed tankard in appreciation of my work on the Committee, and was wished a happy and long retirement by Mr Boothby, the chairman, and all the members. I thanked them for the gift and their kind remarks and wished them continued success for the future.

In December that year, we returned to live in Bristol for the second time. Our eldest daughter, Marianne, still lived there, and had our grandchildren, Neil and Leanne. Jeannette, our youngest daughter, was a nursing sister in Princess Margaret Hospital, Swindon and living in Marlborough, and our middle daughter Lydia was still living at home with us. So, for obvious reasons, we had returned to Bristol.

Sybil had been given a transfer to the Marks and Spencer Store in Broadmead, Bristol, where she had originally started with them. When we were living in Stafford in 1982, my dear mum died, and my dad died in 1986. Back in Bristol, we bought a house in Kingswood, which is on the Wiltshire side of the city and close to the countryside.

Being now retired, and with nothing to do, was absolutely alien to my way of life, so I knew that, if only for sanity's sake, I would have to do something. Working all those years with police dogs, left me no option but to contemplate something to do with dogs. Being so connected with the training of dogs over many years, gave me the experience and confidence to start up on my own, now that the time had come. I had always been aware that there was a need for experienced dog trainers in civilian life, so in April 1988, I started my own dog training business called 'Canine Specialists (International) UK'.

I got myself known by distributing little posters, outlining my experience and qualifications, to veterinary surgeons in Bristol, Bath and the surrounding areas, the result of which kept me quite busy. Much of my work involved advising owners of dogs with behavioural problems, on referral from veterinary surgeons. I used the only method which I believe to be successful: training the owner along with the dog. I would refuse point blank to train any dog without the owner being present.

Later, I had a block advert in Yellow Pages, which greatly increased my work load and took me further afield. I suspect that I am going to step on many people's toes making this statement, but I do so with no disrespect to anyone, and, more so, because it's a fact. There is much ignorance among people in the dog world, and I use that word in the nicest possible way.

Over the years, I have found that the first and biggest mistake that many dog owners make is that they treat their dogs as if they were human beings. Believe me, if the dogs could talk, they would not thank you for that. All forms of training should be based, not on treating the dog as an intelligent being with sense of duty, but as an animal, unable to discriminate between good or bad, right or wrong, and without any moral values. A dog does not learn by logical thinking, but by association, and through the faculty of memory. By treating the dog in this manner, one is not asking it to do anything beyond its powers of comprehension, and the dog (and the owner) is spared much suffering.

Shortly after I returned to Bristol, I had a letter from a practice of solicitors in Lancashire, who were in the process of publishing a register of expert witnesses.

They said that they had been given my name by a Chief Constable, as a person suitably qualified and experienced to give expert opinion on matters relating to dog behaviour. They asked if I was prepared to be included in the register and, if so, to send them details of my qualifications, etc. I did this and have been listed in the 'UK Register of Expert Witnesses', since it was first published in 1988.

During that time, I have received instructions from solicitors all over the country, on over 80 occasions, preparing reports and attending courts to give expert evidence. I have been several times on Radio Bristol, speaking on the training and behaviour of dogs, and also on a programme answering questions from listeners, phoning in with problems on dog behaviour.

They were all live calls, not questions which I had been given in advance.

I also trained a German Shepherd dog for a big part in the S4C Television series, 'Glan Hafryn'. Unlike most animal behaviourists. I have no diplomas, nor any letters after my name, but a good working knowledge of how a dog's mind works, learned over many years of close contact with hundreds of dogs, and paying particular attention to their re-actions and behaviour in various situations and at the actual time when any particular behaviour manifests itself.

Not on opinions based when seeing the dog some time later in a completely different environment, in no way related to where the problem originated. I have always believed in the saying, 'There is no substitute for experience'.

162

Thinking that it was about time that I took things a little easier, and having been in hospital for two operations, I closed my dog training business in February 1995, but I still continued to act as an expert witness. Even now, people often telephone me to ask my advice on any behavioural problem they may have with their dogs. I don't mind this, it's them that's paying for the telephone call, and I'm prepared to chat to them and give them advice, for as long as they like Pembrokeshire Police ceased to exist in 1968, when they amalgamated with Cardigan and Carmarthen Police and Mid Wales Police, to become Dyfed Powys Police. A few years later Pembrokeshire Police Officers Association was formed, and we meet at Haverfordwest twice a year. In June, we have our annual general meeting and, in November, we have our Reunion

Dinner for members and their spouses. In 1997, I was elected chairman of the Association.

Pembrokeshire Police was always like one big family, everyone knew everyone else, and now we can meet twice a year to renew our friendships and reminisce on old times. It is a unique Association in as much that it continues to get smaller as time goes by. It is inevitable that the day will come when there are none of us left, but I am sure that the reputation of the Pembrokeshire Police will continue to be talked about long after we are all gone.

Since Sybil and I came back to Bristol, we have been blessed with two more grandchildren.

Our youngest daughter, Jeannette, who is a diabetic specialist sister in Salisbury Hospital, and her husband Steven, have given us Harriet, who is now 7 years, and Edward who is 5 years.

They still live in Marlborough, which is about 45 minutes journey from us. Marianne is a qualified nursery nurse. Her son Neil, is now 19 years, and is in the Army. After two years in the Army Apprentice College, he is now in the Royal Signals and has just returned from a tour in Bosnia. Her daughter Leanne, is 17, and is in college studying Drama and Performing Arts. Lydia, our middle daughter, still lives at home and works in a Residential Home for the Elderly.

Yes, much water has passed under the bridge since those far off days, when I used to spend hours watering the tomato plants in my dad's nursery. Amongst all those plants in the huge glasshouses, it was like being in a jungle and, although I was doing a job, it felt as if I was not really involved, but it gave me plenty of thinking time. I was never what one might call ambitious, it was just that I wanted to do something that really involved me, something that would spur my competitive spirit, and I have always believed that if something is worth doing, then do it well.

Life has been extremely good to me and for that I thank God. I was fortunate to have good parents, who gave us a good start in life, and I have certainly been blessed with a wonderful wife. Everything that I have done, I have done for her. She has always been so supportive, and as the song says, 'She is the wind beneath my wings' Many people look back and think what changes they would make if they had their life over again. I can honestly say that I don't think that I would want to make any changes. I have had a contented and happy life. I have seen my children grow up, and now my grandchildren. Money has never meant anything to me. Wealth to me means good health, happiness and contentment and, by the grace of God, I have had all three.

Bryn on Police horse, South Yorkshire Lass

Bryn, when he was a Chief Inspector in Stafford

CHAPTER TEN
METHODS OF DOG TRAINING

With over 30 years experience working full time with dogs and for the majority of that time engaged in their training and that of the handlers/owners, I have obviously gained quite an in-depth knowledge into the psychology of the dog.

I am not suggesting that one has to have an in-depth knowledge of dog psychology to be able to train a dog in basic obedience, but it does help if one understands how a dogs mind works.

Many good books have been written about dog training but often without the nitty-gritty on how actually to teach the dog to carry out the commands it is given.

The first important thing is to get the full confidence of your dog. All future training depends on it. Never chastise your dog unnecessarily, only immediately it does something wrong. Never if you are not sure that the dog understood perfectly what was wanted of it. Chastisement means a loud 'No' and never physical punishment.

Because dogs have such acute senses, such as those of scent and hearing and with a capacity to learn, owners tend to assume that a dog's intelligence equals that of a human being. The dog is often credited with reasoning powers and an understanding of human behaviour and morality.

Owners that think along these lines prevent themselves from recognising the unbridgable mental gap that exists between man and dog.

One must use a form of training which treats the dog not as an intelligent human being imbued with a sense of duty, but as an animal beyond good or evil, living in a world without moral values and learning not by logical thinking but by association and through the faculty of memory. By teaching the dog in this manner, we are not asking it to do anything beyond its powers of comprehension and the dog and its owner is spared much suffering and disappointment, while the enjoyment of both pupil and trainer is facilitated and increased.

167

Be decisive in your commands, firm and most important of all, be sure that you know exactly what you want the dog to do and how it should be done. Never try to teach the dog anything until you yourself have a thorough knowledge of how to teach it and a clear mental picture of every stage of the training. Above all, never attempt anything if you have the slightest fear of getting 'lost'. Reward everything that is well done by the dog and always finish a period of training on a good note. Never leave off if the dog has done something wrong, and do not continue a training period for such a long time that the dog becomes tired and bored. Make it do something it enjoys and then finish.

The sooner you can start training the dog the better. Teaching the dog in its early life does much to prevent it developing any bad habits. It will pay to remember that there are no short cuts to dog training; trying to rush things can only have the effect of un-doing hours of hard work. For the first couple of weeks of the training, try to do it in a quiet area where there are no distractions to take the dogs attention from what you are teaching it. As the dog gets more accustomed to the training sessions and gains in confidence, you can then carry out the training in areas where there are other people and animals moving about in the vicinity. By this stage the dog will be able to concentrate more fully on what you are teaching it and will have very much more confidence in dealing with the exercises.

In this short chapter I will concentrate on the few simple exercises which, after all, are the basis of obedience and will help dog owners to get the maximum enjoyment out of their dogs. These exercises are: teaching your dog to walk at your side properly whilst on the lead, teaching the dog, on command, to go into the 'down', 'sit' and 'stay' positions, and to 'come' when called by the handler/owner.

Initial training. The initial training of the dog requires great care and the trainer must be in complete command at all times. It is on this training that the behaviour, responses and control of the finished dog depends.

The lead. The lead should be used to check the dog and NOT punish disobedience. Nothing is worse than to see a dog

168

cringe when its lead is produced. When it is produced, the dog should show pleasure.

Disobedience and faults. Check faults as soon as they occur; never let one pass, as they soon develop into disobedience and produce badly trained dogs, but be very careful to discriminate between disobedience and misunderstanding. By punishing misunderstanding, the dog becomes confused and this simply delays training, because the dog will lose that trust in its trainer, which must be there before any useful training starts. Punishment is administered by tone of voice with a loud 'NO'. Before any punishment, be sure in your own mind that it is disobedience and not misunderstanding; when necessary, it must follow the act immediately. If delay occurs, the act must go unpunished.

Control. The foundation on which all future training will be built is obedience and it will be some time before the trainer has that control off the lead which he enjoys on it. Because of this control, it is possible in the first few weeks to make that foundation sure, but conversely it is possible to spoil good material.

Firmness and nagging. If the trainer continually checks the dog unnecessarily, by use of the lead, eventually the dog will not respond. At all times be firm, but do not 'nag' or be harsh.

Praise. Always be ready to praise good work by patting the dog and saying in a pleased tone of voice, 'Good dog'.

Dog's affection. The more the dog is taught the easier it is to teach. Training makes it receptive, but much useful work can be done by the trainer simply being with the dog. It increases the dog's affection and general knowledge. It is the former which must be obtained before serious training can commence. If it is not obtained the dog does not have that immediate interest on sighting its handler. Gain the dog's affection at all costs.

Commands. The command which one puts into the tone of voice will be reflected in the way in which the dog obeys. Words of command need not be shouted in a loud voice but should be crisp and authoritative. Toneless mumbling will produce sluggish response from the dog. If commands are given crisply, the response will be equally crisp.

Alertness. Remember too, that when out training you must be just as much on the alert as you expect your dog to be. Do not wander, keep your mind on what you are doing, for you can be perfectly sure that unless you are on the alert, your dog's mind will wander to other things, and he, remember, must be checked.

Qualities. Dog trainers must be keen, alert, firm, patient, kind, and above all, have DOG SENSE. All these qualities will be strained to breaking point in one way or another, but whatever happens, tempers must be kept. A quick and thoughtless action can undo many hours of hard work.

Build-up. The dogs training must proceed along lines on which it 'grows up' in its training, just as it does in body. Each stage must be built up thoroughly so that it becomes instinctive and, between the trainer and dog, an invisible but unbreakable bond. To start with, this bond will be visible in the lead; later affection and confidence will take the lead's place.

At all times.

REWARD GOOD WORK
HUMOUR MISUNDERSTANDING
PUNISH disobedience immediately.

Lessons mastered. Once the dog has mastered the rudiments of each lesson and understands what to do on word of command, all lessons can be practised daily, but all previous lessons must be mastered before proceeding further.

Words of command. The same word should always be used for the position the handler wishes the dog to assume, e.g., if the dog has been trained to sit on the command 'SIT', do not use the command 'DROP'. The actual word used is of little importance but try to keep all commands to the dog to single syllable words. Except for imperative commands such as 'SIT', 'DOWN', 'NO', the word of command should be preceded by the name of the dog, e.g. 'JET, COME', with a slight pause between the name of the dog and the command. By doing this, the trainer at once gains the dog's attention before giving it a definite order.

Commands need not be given in a loud voice, indeed they should not, but always clearly and distinctly, putting as much emphasis as possible into the tone. There must be no question of the dog complying with the trainer's requests; they must be commands and obeyed instantly.

Command 'NO'. To be used whenever the dog is doing anything contrary to the wishes of the trainer/owner.

It can only be taught as and when the occasion arises, and there is no set way to teach this.

Whenever the occasion arises, give a sharp pull on the lead and at the same time, a sharp command, 'NO'.

Walking to heel on lead.

(1) Word of command - 'Heel'

(2) Position of dog - Standing on left, shoulder opposite and close to handler's knee.

(3) Handler walks forward at normal pace at the same time saying

(a) "...(name of dog) ... Heel". The dog will recognise it's name and be on the alert, but "Heel" will be meaningless to it.

(b) Any reluctance to follow will be countered by smartly tightening lead and words of encouragement, repeating the dog's name at frequent intervals.

(c) Once the dog follows willingly, position as at (2) will be maintained.

(d) Handler retains lead in right hand, lengthening or shortening lead as necessary.

(e) Frequent halts to be made.

(f) Encouragement given vocally and occasionally by the LEFT hand when the dog behaves correctly and is in the right position.

(g) Check by use of lead if position is not correct.

(h) Always commence with " (name) 'HEEL'.

(i)   Lead to be hanging slack, (U shaped) in front of handlers legs.

(j)   Time for practice - 15 to 20 minutes, two or three times daily for first few days.

Later, introduce right, left and about turns into the walks.

Sitting.

(1) Word of command - 'SIT'.

(2) Position of dog   - Hindquarters and paws of front feet only on ground.

(3) Handler

(a)   Holding lead in right hand only, place left hand with thumb and forefingers extended over loin of dog and press firmly, at the same time placing the right hand UNDER the dogs muzzle pressing upwards and giving the command 'SIT', until the dogs hindquarters are forced to the ground.

(b)   Each time the dog rises, until commanded to do so, repeat (a).

(c)   When dog will sit temporarily, stand up straight, encourage dog as necessary.

(d)   Once the dog sits on command, after standing up straight, gradually move away from the dog to extent of lead, keeping your eye on the dog all the time. If the dog should attempt to rise from the sit, give firm command 'NO', put the dog back into the SIT position, repeating the command 'SIT' as you do so.

(e)   Practice 10 to 20 minutes, three times daily and EVERY time when coming to a halt when walking dog to heel.

Down.

(1)   Word of command - 'DOWN'

(2)   Position of dog - Both fore and hindquarters on the ground, forelegs extended.

(3)   Handler sits the dog by his left side holding lead in right hand only.

(a)   take forelegs of dog together in right hand, placing left hand, thumb and forefinger extended across shoulders just at base of neck, giving the command 'DOWN' at the same time pressing down with left hand until dog is forced to the ground. Whilst having to press down firmly, make sure that no hurt is caused to the dog.

(b)   If dog attempts to rise from position without command, give firm command 'NO' and immediately repeat action at (a).

(c)   Repeat for 10 to 20 minutes two or three times a day until dog assumes correct position on word of command and then as necessary.

(d)   Repeat above until handler can retreat to extent of lead and gradually circle the dog, holding lead at that distance, without the dog moving. Staying in Down position - Handler moving away.

(1)   Word of command - 'STAY'
(2)   Position of dog - As for 'Down'.

(a) With dog in DOWN position, facing handler, hold lead in left hand (Long lead)

(b)   Command the dog 'STAY' with right hand uplifted, palm facing the dog.

(c)   Walk backwards very slowly away from dog to full extent of lead. Should the dog move, instantly chastise it with a firm 'NO', return to dog and place it in the original position, repeating the command 'STAY' and commence again.

(d)   DOG will probably let handler move a few yards away and then suddenly dash away Should it do this, the lead will pull the dog up with a sudden jerk and the handler must give the command 'NO' to coincide with the jerk. Return the dog to original spot and repeat.

(e)   When the dog lies still when the handler moves away, and returns, gradually circle the dog. Later alternate this by walking past the dog at short distances and, later still, by stepping over the dog. Move away and return to the dog from different directions. (At this stage, this is all done whilst still holding the long lead in left hand.

(f)   Repeat 15 to 20 minutes two or three times daily, using fresh areas.

(g)   Eventually, practice with lead not held in hand, but gently laid on ground before moving away from the dog.

(h)   This exercise must be perfect before attempting to work the dog off lead.

Obedience off lead.

Training the dog on the lead, the handler has always been in complete control, but off the lead this control will depend on the thoroughness of previous training, the tone of voice used and the rapport which has been established between dog and handler before training began.

Much, if not all, of the control required can be obtained if the handler has ensured perfection in the 'DOWN' position. It is this exercise that will instil into the dog's brain that the trainer is in complete control at whatever distance he may be away from the dog.

The advance from working the dog on the lead to that of working the dog off the lead must be gradual and cannot be accomplished in one fell swoop. The transition period should be occupied by the trainer gradually moving further and further away from the dog and at all times insisting on immediate compliance to all commands.

All training off the lead should start in an enclosed area, so that the handler need never be in a position where the dog can elude him.

Coming to hand.
Word of command ... 'COME'

This is possibly the most useful part of obedience to teach any dog and can be used on any occasion. It also teaches the

174

dog to approach the handler with head up and tail wagging and not as if expecting punishment, When your dog is running free off the lead remember that it learns by association, so every time the dog comes to you on the command 'COME, caress it and give it plenty of praise, even if it has done something whilst running free. If you ever punish the dog when it returns to your side, it will associate the punishment with returning to you and become 'hand-shy'. When the dog is running free, call it to your side with the command 'COME' at frequent intervals, put the dog on the lead, caress and praise it and then let it free again. If the dog is only called to heel at the end of the free period, it will soon learn that it means the end of it's freedom and will be reluctant to return to the handler on the command 'COME'. When the dog is called to heel at frequent intervals, it will never know when it is the end of the free period.

Remember - a dog is only as good as its handler. Make sure you have a good dog.